Books are to be returned on or before the last date below.

This book must be returned by the last date stamped above.
Rhaid dychwelyd y llyfr hwn erbyn y dyddiad diwethaf a stampiwyd uchod.

A charge will be made for any lost, damaged or overdue books.
Codir tâl os bydd llyfr wedi ei golli neu ei niweidio neu heb ei
ddychwelyd mewn pryd

OFFA'S DYKE PATH NORTH

Knighton to Prestatyn

Ernie and Kathy Kay and Mark Richards

Photographs by Archie Miles
General editor Michael Allaby

AURUM PRESS

COUNTRYSIDE COMMISSION · ORDNANCE SURVEY
COUNTRYSIDE COUNCIL FOR WALES

Acknowledgements for the Second Edition

The whole of the National Trail, and a selection of the circular walks, have been fully resurveyed for this new edition.

Special thanks are due to Jim Saunders, the Offa's Dyke Path Development Officer (for the Countryside Council for Wales and Powys County Council) and to Dave McGlade, his field assistant, for help and advice, especially on Path changes. Also to Mike Wynne Griffith for help on circular walks.

Ernie and Kathy Kay have had an association with the Welsh Border for the past 36 years. They helped plan Offa's Dyke Path and are founder members and officers of the Offa's Dyke Association. They now live right on the Offa's Dyke Path. Mark Richards is well known as an illustrator and author of guide books.

This revised edition first published 1995 by Aurum Press Ltd in association with the Countryside Commission and the Ordnance Survey
Text copyright © 1989, 1995 by Aurum Press Ltd, The Countryside Commission and The Ordnance Survey
Maps Crown copyright © 1989, 1995 by the Ordnance Survey
Photographs copyright © 1989, 1995 by the Countryside Commission

British Library Cataloguing in Publication Data
Kay, Ernie.
Offa's Dyke Path North: Knighton to
Prestatyn. – (National trail guides; 2)
1. Welsh Marches. Long-distance footpaths:
Offa's Dyke Path. Recreations: Walking – Visitors' guides
I. Title II. Kay, Kathy III. Richards, Mark
1949–IV. Series
914.24
ISBN 1 85410 322 9
OS ISBN 0 319 00385 X

Book design by Robert Updegraff
Cover photograph: Knucklas Viaduct and Castle from Offa's Dyke Path
(Archie Miles/Countryside Commission)
Title page photograph: Offa's Dyke above the Ceiriog Valley
The photograph on page 65 is reproduced courtesy of the National Trust
Photographic Library/Erik Pelham

Typeset by Wyvern Typesetting Ltd, Bristol
Printed and bound in Italy by Printer Srl, Trento

CONTENTS

How to use this guide

The 177-mile (285-kilometre) Offa's Dyke Path is covered by two national trail guides. This book features the northern section of the Path, from Knighton to Prestatyn (97 miles/156 kilometres including sections through towns). A companion guide features the Path from Chepstow to Knighton.

The guide is in three parts:

• The introduction, with an historical background to the area and advice for walkers.

• The Path itself, split into seven chapters, with maps opposite the description for each route section. This part of the guide also includes information on places of interest as well as a number of short walks which can be taken around each part of the Path. Key sites are numbered both in the text and on the maps to make it easier to follow the route description.

• The last part includes useful information such as local transport, accommodation and organisations involved with the Path.

The maps have been prepared by the Ordnance Survey for this trail guide using 1:25 000 Pathfinder maps as a base. The line of Offa's Dyke Path is shown in yellow, with the status of each section of the Path – footpath or bridleway, for example – shown in green underneath (see key on inside front cover). These rights of way markings also indicate the precise alignment of the Path, which walkers should follow. In some cases, the yellow line may show a route which is different from that shown on older maps; walkers are recommended to follow the yellow route in this guide, which will be the route that is waymarked with the distinctive acorn symbol ♣ used for all national trails. Some sections of the Path may be shown following a line of black dots, since the base map available at the time of producing this edition does not have up-to-date details of the public rights of way over which Offa's Dyke Path goes. Any parts of the Path that may be difficult to follow on the ground are clearly highlighted in the route description, and important points to watch for are marked with letters in each chapter, both in the text and on the maps. *Some maps start on a right-hand page and continue on the left-hand page – black arrows (➡) at the edge of the maps indicate the start point.*

Should there be a need to divert the Path from the route shown in this guide, for maintenance work or because the route has had to be changed, walkers are advised to follow any waymarks or signs along the Path.

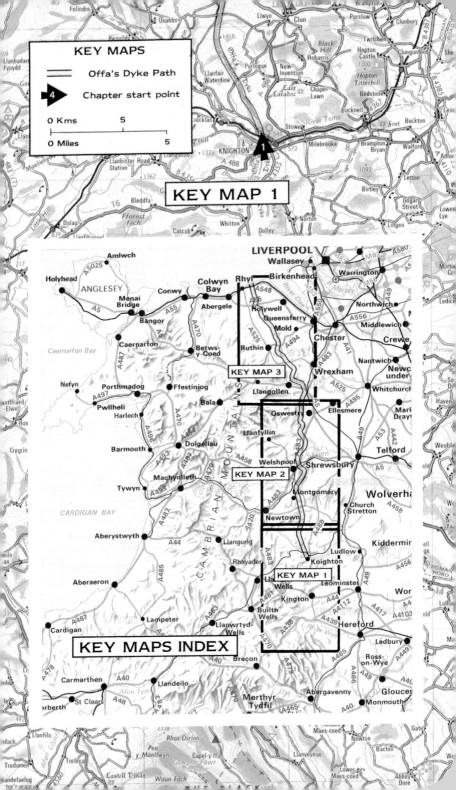

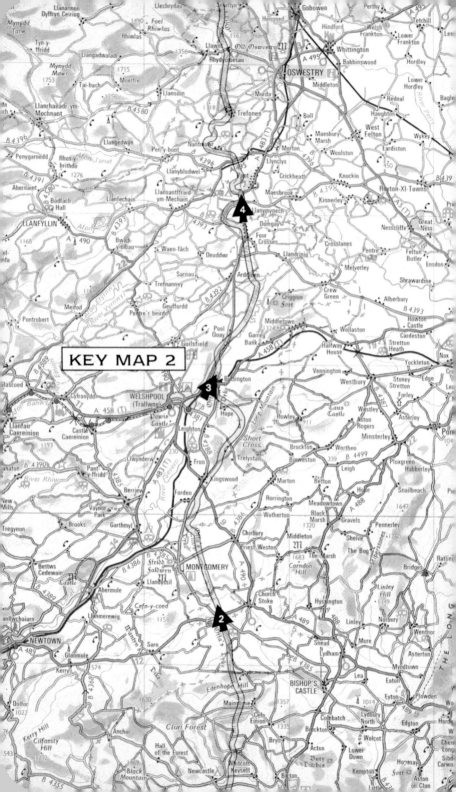

KEY MAP 2

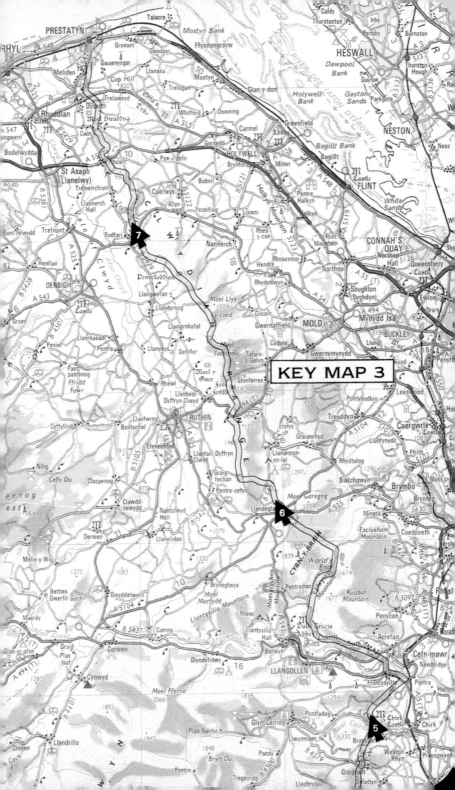

KEY MAP 3

Distance checklist

This list will assist you in calculating the distances between places on the northern half of the Path where you may be planning to stay overnight, or in checking your progress along the way.

location	approx. distance from previous location	
	miles	km
Knighton	0	0
B4368 for Clun	7.3	11.8
Churchtown	3.8	6.1
A489 'Blue Bell' (Brompton Crossroads)	4.0	6.4
B4386 for Montgomery	2.9	4.7
A490/B4388 junction for Forden	3.3	5.3
Buttington	6.1	9.8
Pool Quay	2.0	3.2
Llanymynech	8.5	13.7
Trefonen	5.9	9.5
B4580 for Oswestry	3.0	4.8
B4500 for Chirk Castle	5.0	8.1
Froncysyllte	4.2	6.8
Dinas Bran/Llangollen turn	3.6	5.8
World's End	3.7	6.0
Llandegla (centre of village)	4.0	6.4
A494 'Clwyd Gate'	6.1	9.8
Jubilee Tower, Clwydian Hills	4.1	6.6
Bodfari	7.5	12.1
Rhuallt	4.3	7.0
Prestatyn	7.6	12.2

PREFACE

National trails are an enticement. Every time I see a new one on the map I want to walk it. They will lead you out into your countryside on a natural line. Some of the upland paths are rooted in our history: the 'green roads' of England and Wales.

Trails like Offa's Dyke are particularly suited for long journeys, but they can also be tried out on an afternoon or over a weekend. Or use them as part of a round trip, or circular walk; suggestions for these are included in this guide. National trails are maintained by local authorities on behalf of the Countryside Commission and the Countryside Council for Wales, and are well waymarked with our distinctive acorn. Each trail provides a good, and sometimes challenging, walk or ride in the countryside.

I hope that you will go and make the most of them, using this guide to keep you on the correct route and to add to your enjoyment of the countryside and understanding of the area.

Sir John Johnson
Chairman
Countryside Commission

Foreword

by Lord Hunt of Llanfair Waterdine, KG

I treasure the memory of a hot summer's day in July 1971 when, at my home town of Knighton, I declared open the long distance route along the line of Offa's Dyke, at the invitation of the Countryside Commission. For my wife and myself this marked a high point in our long association with the Welsh Border, which had begun nearly thirty years earlier. It was, indeed, almost (but not quite!) as memorable a moment as the welcome I received in the town and in our parish of Llanfair Waterdine after my return from Everest in 1953. The Dyke itself follows the high ground just above our old home and our present cottage in the parish, so the reader will, I hope, forgive me, as a past-President of the Offa's Dyke Association, for feeling especially sentimental, almost proprietorial, about the Dyke. I have sampled many other national trails; each has its special attractions, but the Offa's Dyke Path holds pride of place in my affections.

To celebrate the opening event, we set off that same day in 1971 on a four-day trek northwards towards the terminus of the Dyke Path at Prestatyn; the prevailing heatwave and the bracken flies detracted not at all from a journey which, for us, held some of the illusory magic of trail-blazing. As so often in a busy life, time was our enemy; it was only a year later that we were able to complete our acquaintance with the Dyke by walking southwards, from Spoad Farm in the valley of the Clun, to reach its end on the red cliffs overlooking the River Severn.

But more important than this personal connection is the link which the Dyke provides with the distant past in the story of our nation. Often, standing on Llanfair hill above our cottage, I have had a strong sense of a dim, unrecorded age, before invaders from across the North Sea forced our Celtic ancestors westwards into Wales. Long before King Offa caused the construction of his monumental earthwork, I seem to perceive, through the mists of time, those tribal people in their upland dwellings who grew corn on the high ground and hunted deer and wild boar in the densely forested Teme Valley down below. I have, too, a sense of that still-distant but recorded past; of the wars and skirmishes between Romans and Celts, Normans and Welshmen, which were fought around the hill forts and castles which provide one of the main attractions of this national trail. Indeed, I believe that it is not mere fantasy to suggest that, while walking along Offa's Dyke, the past is still with us in the present.

However this may be, I hope that readers of this guidebook will share my own delight in the scenery it affords and the ancient history which it conjures up.

John Hunt

The limestone crags of the Eglwyseg, below which Offa's Dyke Path runs.

PART ONE

INTRODUCTION

'Not the oldest, nor the longest, but the best.' So said Lord Sandford about the Offa's Dyke Path at an Annual General Meeting of the Offa's Dyke Association, of which he was then President. This Path is based not on a geographical feature, but on a man-made historic one, and to this it owes the variety of its scenery. It may not have the high lonely moorland of the Pennine Way, nor the sparkling sea views of the coastal paths, but it is unique in the different kinds of countryside through which it passes and the strange stories of the past told by the historic features seen on the way.

Historical background: a frontier zone

The Welsh Border, though it has not always been a frontier in the modern sense, lies along the division between the Welsh uplands to the west and the lower ground of the English Midlands to the east. There is no single edge, but a variety of hills, so the exact position of this boundary has varied from age to age.

Early peoples would not have formed the concept of a boundary line; nevertheless, this area often acted as a division between peoples who felt a need to protect themselves from neighbours of different origin. Thus some of the most striking early signs of occupation on the hilltops are the hill forts, which are very numerous throughout the Border and include some of the largest and most complex fortifications found anywhere in the world. They are usually thought to date from the Iron Age, just before the Roman invasion of Britain, but recent investigations show that some originated in the Bronze Age, as long ago as 1200 BC, with some ramparts dating back to 800 BC, and occupation sometimes lasting for more than 1,000 years. The forts were certainly still in use for native defence against the Romans: somewhere in these Border hills Caractacus must have made his last stand before being taken as a captive to Rome, but we cannot be sure exactly where.

The Romans themselves also left their mark on the area, with remains of forts, roads and other structures, but they pushed on westwards without establishing any boundary feature as they had at Hadrian's Wall. The first marked line must be the feature that most concerns us on this Path, Offa's Dyke itself – believed to date from the late 8th century – but of this more later.

The Border remained an area of conflict. William the Conqueror must have recognised the threat, for he made grants of land to powerful 'Marcher' barons, who built defensive castles in the area known as the Welsh 'Marches'. The word 'Marches' comes from the same origin as 'Mark', possibly referring to Offa's Dyke itself. It does not refer to walking, or the season of the year and certainly not to damp marshland! Norman lords, and their successors until the late 15th century, the 'Lords Marchers' (who are not a cricket team raising money for charity), were granted lands in the Welsh Border area. Many claimed special rights, not subject to the normal restraints of English law, over a wide, imprecise area which they held and ruled by right of conquest. Their castles range from the numerous earth mounds of the 'motte and bailey' type to great stone buildings, still forbidding after seven or eight centuries of neglect and decay, such as Chepstow and Rhuddlan. The Welsh fought back and there was frequent Border conflict until the defeat of Owain Glyndwr in 1410. They built castles too; Dinas Bran, above Llangollen, is the most impressive you will see.

Castell Dinas Bran – a 13th century Welsh stronghold.

With the castles came other features that still survive. The Marcher strongholds were often accompanied by the establishment of a 'borough', usually a planned town. Some decayed, some never developed, but many tiny villages still retain a complicated grid layout. For the common people, the nearest refuge in case of alarm was usually the church, often built with a strong defensive 'Border' tower. Many of these have survived, while the rest of the medieval fabric has decayed or been replaced by something more fashionable.

In later centuries, the hills which had divided peoples were important for minerals and water power, and many parts of the Border became important centres of early industry. Some of these still survive, particularly east of the Clwydian Hills; elsewhere the remains of mills, tramways and minepits survive in areas from which the bustle of industry has long departed.

From the times of peace. many graceful domestic buildings also remain, ranging from stately mansions to the timber-framed farmhouses and cottages for which much of the Border is noted.

Offa's Dyke – when, where, why and how?

For over half its length the Path keeps company with the Dyke that gives it its name. Sometimes it is a great bank up to 25 feet (7.6 metres) high, with a deep ditch to the west; at other times it is no more than a hedgebank or a ridge across a ploughed field, identifiable only because it is 'in the right place'. In some parts where you might expect to find it, for instance in the quite low-lying areas north of Monmouth, the Dyke seems not to be there at all. This unpredictability has led to much scholarly speculation and dispute about the Dyke.

When was it built? Strangely, no contemporary records relating to its construction or early use have been found. The first positive reference comes about 100 years after the attributed date of construction, when Asser, Bishop of Sherborne but previously from Wales, tells us positively that King Offa ordered a great Dyke to be built between Wales and Mercia, stretching from sea to sea. The lack of contemporary mention has caused some to doubt whether Offa did indeed build the Dyke, or whether it may have existed earlier. However, there seems little reason to doubt the later records, tradition and the evidence of place names on the line. After the Romans, Offa was probably the first ruler to have the power and organisation to carry out work on this scale, and the appearance and alignment of the whole earthwork suggest that it must have been conceived as a whole.

Having said this, it may seem strange that there should be any doubt about *where* the Dyke runs. The most problematical area is in the north, where recent excavation has thrown doubt on whether any of the fragmentary remains north of Treuddyn, identified by Sir Cyril Fox in his monumental survey of the earthwork in the 1920s and 1930s, are in fact part of the Dyke. As a result, Dr David Hill of Manchester University, who has directed the work in this area, has concluded that the other Dyke further to the east, known as Wat's Dyke, might well be the northern section of Offa's. Elsewhere, the doubtful areas are smaller, usually relating to gaps or stretches of 'hedgebank' type dyke. In the southern parts, where Fox often attributed the absence of dyke to impenetrable forest, Frank Noble's detailed studies identified traces in several areas where it had been thought missing, as well as explaining certain of the gaps. David Hill now considers that all stretches south of Bridge Sollers on the Wye may be a different earthwork.

Why was the Dyke built? Fox's view was that it was a boundary marker rather than an actual defensive work. However, both Hill and Noble, in their detailed studies, eventually concluded that the form and siting of the Dyke pointed to defence, possibly with added fortifications, such as a stockade, and with the intention of permanent manning. Suggestions that the Dyke might have been an ancient trackway are quite at odds with its profile and the steep gradients it traverses.

As to *how* it was constructed, the controversial questions are whether the Dyke was built from end to end by a single expert construction team, or whether local gangs of workers were responsible for their individual stretches. The second theory would explain some of the odd anomalies, such as the strange right-angled bends at Hergan where two teams may have failed to meet, or the abrupt change from high dyke to low bank on the hill just south of Knighton. However, there is no certain evidence.

The landscape along the Path

Because Offa's Dyke and its Path do not follow a single natural feature, they pass through a succession of landscape forms of great variety. These are derived from the underlying rocks and support an equal variety of types of natural vegetation and farming activity.

Looking down on the River Dee from the Pont Cysyllte Aqueduct.

In the far south the Path is high on the eastern edge of the spectacular limestone cliffs of the lower Wye Valley which form the western edge of the Forest of Dean plateau, an area rich in coal and other minerals and one of the earliest industrial areas. Rocks of the older Devonian age underlie most of the route from Monmouth to Hay but produce two very different land forms; the rolling farmlands of the Monnow and Trothy Valleys and then the spectacular hills of the Black Mountains, supporting only a few sheep and ponies.

The northbound walker follows the north–south 'grain' of the landscape up to Hay, while north of the upper Wye Valley for a long way the lie of the land is east–west over a terrain formed from the underlying Silurian rocks. Landforms again vary from rounded moorlands such as Hergest Ridge and grassy hills such as Hawthorn, Llanfair and Long Mountain, supporting mainly sheep and, increasingly, conifers, to the fertile river valleys of the Arrow, Lugg, Teme, Caebitra and Camlad where cattle flourish. Many of the Silurian rocks are shales producing a building stone that crumbles with age. You will see many buildings constructed of this material falling into ruin. An example is the old primary school at Knighton, now the Offa's Dyke Centre. The youth hostel in the same building is currently (1995) closed pending structural repairs.

Below Long Mountain the Severn is crossed and its flat alluvial valley, good for cattle but liable to flooding, is followed north to Llanymynech. Seen to the east are the volcanic Breidden Hills. Beyond Llanymynech the Path rises again on the west edge of hills of Carboniferous rocks which produce both the industrial landscapes of west Shropshire and the spectacular limestone crags of the Eglwyseg above Llangollen and the Dee Valley.

A short stretch of peaty moorland, increasingly under conifers, is crossed south of Llandegla and the Path then climbs on to the barren north–south moors of the Clwydian Hills, another Silurian ridge. This is sandwiched between the alluvial Clwyd Vale to the west, with the volcanic summits of Snowdonia seen beyond, and the Flintshire–Wrexham industrial area, based on Carboniferous Limestone and Coal Measures, to the east. The Dyke itself, but not the Path, goes right through this industrial belt. In its final section the Path is on Carboniferous rocks in a mixed area of moors, pastures and woods until you reach high cliffs above the sands of the North Wales coast.

This description can give only a very simplified account of a complex geological pattern. The way this is reflected in the scenery is evident to the walker. The natural landscape determines the land use pattern, though the extent of new commercial forestry varies. In the long-established 'scenic' areas, such as the Black Mountains and Clwydian Hills, there has been a determined attempt to keep at least the hilltops free of trees. These areas are the only ones on the route where real hill farming (usually sheep, though ponies are often grazed) is extensive. Elsewhere farms are being amalgamated, with some dereliction of buildings and removal of hedges, but less so than in many parts of the country. Small fields for livestock still predominate, resulting in the plethora of stiles for which Offa's Dyke Path is 'famous'. It is still too early to tell what the effects will be of current government policies to reduce numbers of cattle and take land out of agricultural production.

The origins and management of the Path

The idea of national trails, as they are called today, was set out in the National Parks and Access to the Countryside Act 1949, and Offa's Dyke was among the first to be suggested, but the whole idea took some time to get under way. The first trail, the Pennine Way, was not opened officially until 1965. Bodies such as the Ramblers' Association and local activists, including the newly founded Offa's Dyke Association, campaigned for the speedy opening of the other suggested paths. A certain amount of informal waymarking and clearance took place – some of us have unforgettable memories of going round with sickles and wax markers in areas which were then quite impenetrable and are now wide pathways!

All this activity apparently impressed the Countryside Commission, most of the outstanding negotiations were expedited, and the county councils, as agents of the Commission, were enjoined to erect stiles and waymarks along the route. Eventually all this bore fruit at an opening ceremony on 10th July 1971, which was performed by Lord Hunt in the presence of the Chairman of the Countryside Commission, two government ministers, many local dignitaries and the largest crowd ever known to have assembled in the small Border town of Knighton.

Of course, more work remained to be done, and there is a continuing need for maintenance. Some 'permissive' stretches of Path have been made rights of way, Diversion Orders have been put into effect and many of the original stiles and way-marks have been replaced. Volunteers from the Offa's Dyke Association watch over conditions on every stretch of the route, report major problems and carry out minor works themselves. When the Countryside Council for Wales took over the Countryside Commission's responsibilities in the principality in 1991 it also became the body that co-ordinated the management of the Path, two-thirds of which is on the Welsh side of the border. The Council also took over from the Commission the funding of a full-time Offa's Dyke Development Officer (and, more recently, of an assistant) based in Knighton, who works closely with the Association to maintain and promote the Path, in conjunction with the local authorities.

How to walk the Path

Waymarking. Each county highway authority chooses its own design of stiles and signs, so you will find considerable variation as you walk. Several types of marker are in use: wooden, and in some cases, metal, fingerposts; concrete signs (sometimes irreverently described as 'tombstones' or even 'hydrants'

People and dogs on the Path near Orseddwen.

because of their appearance); coloured arrows attached to, or painted on, fences and stiles; and acorns, the universal sign of a national trail, which are usually found on the stiles themselves. 'Usually' because, although all stiles were intended to be so identified, there have been occasional unofficial replacements by farmers, and also because the original metal symbols have proved irresistible to some unprincipled souvenir hunters.

Where the route is unclear, for instance at a junction of paths, you should find a sign to set you on your way, but, although a few walkers claim to have walked on waymarks alone, we do not recommend this. If you also use the maps and description in this book, you should have no difficulty in finding the way.

Do not think, because the Path seldom rises to mountainous heights, that you are in for an easy stroll. In many parts, of which the 'Switchback' stretch north of Knighton is most notorious, the repeated rises and falls on the route mean that in the course of an average day's walk you climb the equivalent of a very considerable mountain. Do not discount the stiles, either!

The surface, too, is very variable, and in some places makes walking difficult, such as on the boggy tops of the Black Mountains and the moors south of Llandegla, on steep slopes in many parts which become slippery in wet weather and are slow to dry out, and on some rough stony stretches in areas such as the Clwydian Hills.

The circular walks suggested at the ends of the sections are *not* part of the official national trail and are unlikely to be signed or maintained to the same standard. You should be prepared to follow the map with great care when walking any of these.

Pleasures along the way

Having described the drawbacks, it is time to explain why, in spite of them, this Path is, as Lord Sandford said, the best. We have referred to the variety of landscape through which it passes, based on different geological formations, including hard sandstones and shales, limestone and the recent soft deposits of river flood plains. On the Black Mountains and the Clwydian Hills you can feel on top of the world, with views of more than 30 miles in every direction on a clear day. The lowland stretches have their views, too; not so wide-ranging, of course, but the Breidden Hills seen across the Severn, or the hills crowding in on the Wye Valley if you have chosen to follow the river, give you a detailed view of a contrasting landscape. No doubt you will feel an urge to explore these other hills laid out before you, and this is as it should be – in walking, as in other activities, one good thing leads to another. The Offa's Dyke Path may have its own special and unequalled beauties, but it also offers a tantalising prospect of adjacent areas of countryside that are well worth visiting.

It is not just the distant views that will divert you from the Path. Continually you will see or hear of buildings, historical and natural sites, or villages and small towns, within reach that you will want to visit. Though this book is divided into sections, each of which can be a comfortable day's walk between convenient stopping places, this arrangement is by no means the only way to walk the Path. It can be walked comfortably in about two weeks, but it is even better to allow extra time for some diversions – two hours for a walk down to Llanthony Abbey, half a day to see Denbigh, or even a day to climb Skirrid or the Breiddens.

This is also a splendid trail for the wildlife enthusiast with a little time to spare. Because of the variety of terrain covered by the Path, and its route through remote and sparsely populated country, a very wide range of species occurs. Recently compiled lists include up to 90 different birds, over 150 wild plant species (identified in a single day and a small area), 12 different butterflies and (in Radnorshire alone) 31 mammals, including nine species of bat, and eight amphibians or reptiles. Obviously we cannot list them all: some have been noted in the text to give local colour, particularly in relation to a season. We have taken care not to identify particular badger sites along the Path because of the problems with illegal hunting.

The Welsh Border has different beauties in each season: even winter is not very severe and the higher land to the west moderates the rainfall. Autumn colour is very fine and the moorlands when the heather is out are a special joy. Spring is a particularly good season to walk, for the variety of flowers then is especially wide, better views occur and birds are more easily seen before the trees are fully out.

This is a Path to linger over, and return to. There is a fine sense of achievement in arriving at Prestatyn seafront or Sedbury Cliffs, but the real pleasures are to be found on the way. Here you can understand why R. L. Stevenson could say, as he wandered through the Cevennes, in France, with a donkey to carry his pack (no stiles!): 'For my part, I travel not to go anywhere, but to go. I travel for travel's sake.'

PART TWO

OFFA'S DYKE PATH NORTH
Knighton to Prestatyn

1 Knighton to Brompton Crossroads

through Churchtown
15 miles (24 km)

This is the toughest part of the whole route though you hardly go above 1,400 feet (425 metres). The grain of the country is east–west so you follow a long procession of short steep climbs and descents. The term 'switchback', relating to this part of the trail, was coined when we were pioneering the route; it has stuck and justly so. However, it is rewarding scenically (most of this section goes through the Shropshire Hills Area of Outstanding Natural Beauty) and quite unspoilt. This area was designated in 1988 as an 'environmentally sensitive area' (ESA) by the Ministry of Agriculture. If you are fit and lucky with the weather, you will have a good day!

In Knighton **1** climb up Broad Street, past the clock tower, and continue on West Street to the former primary school **2**, now a centre of Offa's Dyke activities (see page 38). The Path crosses the recreation ground and 'Offa's Dyke' children's play park beneath: note the coronation 'ER' planting in Kinsley Woods opposite **3**. A sign points to a good stretch of Dyke just off the route which also has the Stone which commemorates the opening of the Path by Lord Hunt. The Path goes through Pinner's Hole beneath the Dyke and descends to the picnic site by the River Teme. This is generally thought to be the Shropshire–Powys boundary, but *here* you are in England as the boundary marks an old course of the river!

Use the riverside and cross the river on the footbridge by the Swansea to Shrewsbury railway. This bridge was hurriedly put up with army help just before the opening of the Path. Go out to the road by Panpunton Farm and immediately opposite start the climb up the hill of the same name. It is steeper than it looks and has caught out many Path walkers who have slept and eaten well in Knighton before starting north **A**. At the top of the 400-foot (120-metre) climb you reach the Dyke again and turn sharply north-west to follow under and by it. It is uncertain what course it followed between the centre of Knighton and this point. Continue the climb to reach the summit ridge of Panpunton Hill. Pause here by the seat dedicated to Frank

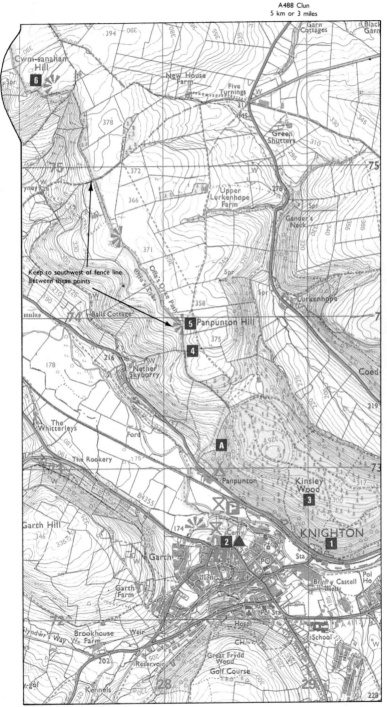

Keep to southwest of fence line
between these points

Contours are given in metres
The vertical interval is 5m

Noble of the Offa's Dyke Association and the cairn in memory of Roy Waters of the Tref y Clawdd (Knighton) Society, who did so much to open the Path. The view from here **4** is back to Knighton and west to the Teme in its valley, with the Gothic arches of the viaduct at Knucklas at its top end.

The Path contours just under the Dyke for 1¼ miles (2 km) beyond the top of Panpunton. The view below is largely of the Teme Valley with Beacon Hill peering over the ridge beyond it: the feeling is of being on top of the world **5**! Eventually you reach and go round the head of a deep cwm with a farm road dropping steeply to the west. Beyond is Cwm-sanaham Hill, reached by climbing steeply through pines and then swinging west to the summit.

From the top of the hill, at 1,343 feet (409 metres), the new views are of the Dyke going north over Llanfair Hill, and of Kerry Hill ridge and Corndon Hill beyond: all pleasures to come **6**. But just before the trig point your route turns north: do *not* go straight on in the same direction. Descend by the edge of two fields, keeping the fence on your right, and then, where the fence turns east, continue ahead to a stile at the top of a dingle. Cross this and drop very steeply through gorse and on the line of the Dyke to a cottage, Brynorgan, seen far below. Give way to anyone you meet coming up the hill – they will be breathless **B**! Pass the cottage and walk out to the minor road beyond by a drive on *top* of the Dyke bank. Watch out for buzzards!

A stile leads to a sharp climb up a rocky outcrop and a descent across two muddy rivulets: the Dyke keeps the same straight course. Do not divert to any of the farm tracks that offer more gentle routes **C**. The stream crossings are fine places for marsh marigolds. The streams themselves have been less of an obstacle to walkers since 1985, when the Offa's Dyke Development Officer at Knighton enlisted the help of the Royal Engineers who were keen to do a training exercise in bridge-building.

The Path then crosses the road by Garbett Hall and goes through a gate beside it. A water tap here is useful. There is a bridleway by the Path for the next 3 miles (5 km), but the two routes do not always coincide. The farm track ahead is used by both, with the Dyke, on a massive scale, just to the east. At another gate the walker climbs on to and up with the Dyke through old pines and larches which suffered badly in storms a few winters ago. The rider stays on the track to the east: both lead up towards the summit of Llanfair Hill.

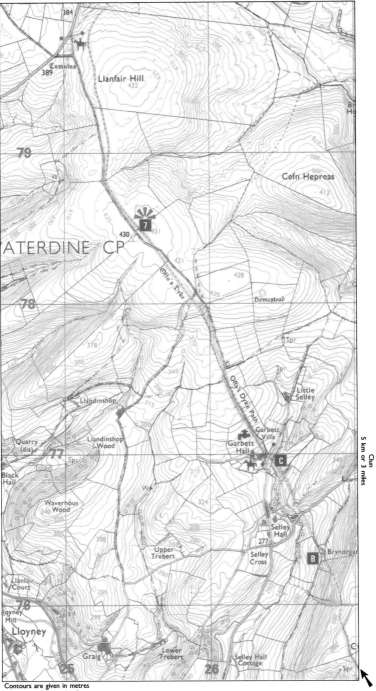

Contours are given in metres
The vertical interval is 5m

When those who know Offa's Dyke well are asked by the less fortunate where they can see 'the best bit', the answer has to be Llanfair Hill rising to Springhill. Once up the rise from Garbett Hall the prospect before you is of open sheep-grazing country with the massive banks and west ditch of the Dyke marching on across the undulations 7. You soon reach the highest point on the Path that is actually on the earthwork, at 1,408 feet (429 metres), but you then drop very little. Some distance on you are asked to leave the Dyke and use the byway just to the west, even though a right of way continues on the top at this point. This is little loss, as the profile view of the banks is just as interesting and the Dyke here does need protection from mass walking. A favourite memory of this stretch is of an Offa's Dyke Association 'AGM Walk' led by Lord Hunt that was so popular, no doubt because of its star attraction, that the queue to cross stretched from one stile to the next.

Two miles from Garbett Hall the byway comes out on to a minor road and follows this up to the crossroads with Springhill Farm just to the east. Turn east, pass the farm and Dyke, and soon turn north by a little wood, crammed with snowdrops at the end of winter. Soon the way goes steeply down a very muddy farm road with the Dyke beyond the fence on the left (west) D. Then go through a gate and the rest of the descent to and through the farmyard of Lower Spoad is on the Dyke. The view to Clun Valley and Graig Hill, with Corndon showing beyond, is impressive. The farmhouse is medieval and its special treasure is an Elizabethan carved hunting scene over the fireplace 8. The house is by the B4368. To the west is the hamlet of Newcastle, which has a pub, the Crown, and 3 miles (5 km) east is Clun 9, a small town with a magnificent Norman castle and a fortress-like church. The Path continues north down fields by the Dyke to the River Clun.

Cross the Clun in front of the splendid half-timbered farm of Bryndrinog, one of the most photographed houses on the Path 10. Go through the farmyard and return to the Dyke just before it crosses the minor Newcastle to Bicton road. The Crown at Newcastle is only just over half a mile to the west by this road. Now the real climbing begins, so a drink at the water tap just beyond the road is recommended. The rise by the Dyke is steep E, with an even steeper fall away to the west. Drop a little to a minor valley, then rise even more sharply to the ridge of Graig Hill through a stand of larches growing on the Dyke bank. At one of the necessary pauses, turn and admire the Dyke

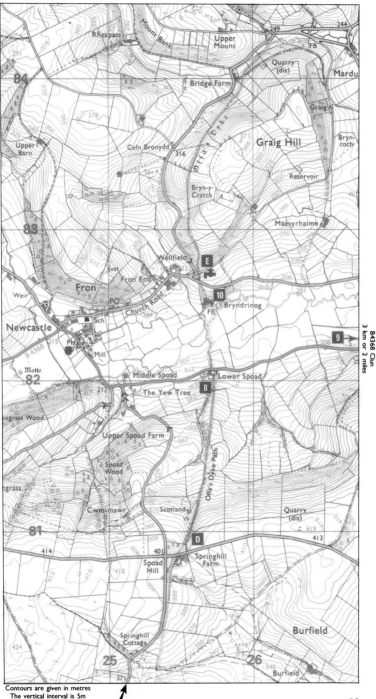

Contours are given in metres
The vertical interval is 5m

33

swooping down Spoad Hill across the Clun. The descent on the far side, still by the Dyke, is more gentle. A muddy dell, below a spring, has to be crossed. Cross the track to Bridge Farm, below you, then a gradual descent through fields and over a footbridge and a stile leads to the road just south of the T-junction at the west end of Mardu. (Make sure you follow the road north-east, not the Dyke, briefly at this point.)

Turn west at the T-junction and immediately fork north-west by a cottage. Go through an iron gate; a further fork takes you back above the Dyke to climb the shoulder of the rise to Hergan. A steep descent, another ascent and a gentler climb take you to a small road by a right-angled bend at Hergan. Cross the road and take the lower of the two paths opposite, then walk a few yards on the Dyke till it bends sharply to the north-west. The northern continuation of the earthwork is well over to the west and the east–west stretch just bridges the gap. Did two construction gangs simply fail to meet? An 1,100-year-old mystery **11**! Follow the Dyke, soon crossing to its western side. The next section, of half a mile, climbs steeply, but with an intermediate drop, to the children's home, formerly a farm, at Middle Knuck.

Keeping west of the buildings, go down to a footbridge, then climb again to the minor road on Knuck Bank. All this climbing has taken you here to only 1,325 feet (404 metres). A major descent follows, by the Dyke and soon in the conifers of Churchtown Wood. We, in describing – and you, in walking – must concentrate on the intricacies of the route: the views are extensive only at the top of each climb.

Coming out of Churchtown Wood your target is the little church of St John's, Churchtown **12**. This serves Mainstone, but even this hamlet is a mile to the east and the church in its deep valley has only a farm for company. The Dyke swoops down to it from both north and south and the walker going north then faces the steepest climb on the whole of the 'switchback', well over 350 feet (100 metres) in only quarter of a mile (400 metres), to a cross track **F**.

Here go west, then immediately north, continuing to climb, but more gently now, to the top of Edenhope Hill and a surfaced lane. Once again there is a steep fall, this time to the isolated upper valley of the River Unk **13**. A substantial bridge crosses the stream where the Dyke temporarily peters out and you then strike north-west on an old cart track to the next stile, by the Dyke at the start of the next climb **G** – the last one for some while!

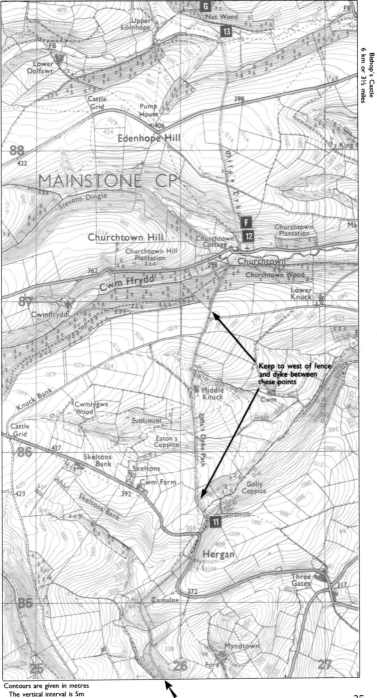

Keep to west of fence and dyke between these points

Contours are given in metres
The vertical interval is 5m

35

Yet again, follow the bank of the Dyke, now up the slope of Nut Wood. At the top of the trees the way is first above, then in, the ditch of the Dyke until you pass by a pond with an island and wildfowl.

Cross two more stiles, and pass another of the gaps in the Dyke with inturned banks (possible 'traffic control' points) to reach the old drove road on the top of the Kerry Hills **14**. This ridge has been a visible target for many miles from the south and it is equally so from the north: a long, unbroken east–west route, extremely suitable for driving cattle from Wales to the English markets in the pre-railway era. It has, at several points, its own cross-ridge short defensive earthworks, which may predate Offa's Dyke: there is a hill fort a little to the east of the point at which you cross it and a small castle site further off, on the way to the former smallest borough in England, Bishop's Castle. The ridge also forms the England–Wales border, here running east to west.

It is 1¼ miles (2 km) and a drop of 600 feet (180 metres) to Mellington and the start of the Montgomery Plain. Follow an exceptionally high stretch of Dyke, first on a drive to its west and then, past Crowsnest cottage, and over a stile, on the earthwork itself. The mass of Corndon Hill dominates the view to the north-east **15**, as you drop quickly to reach a road after more than half a mile. Continue down this road, with the Dyke as its high bank, first to the west side, then the east, and then to the west again **16**. This extra height allows a splendid display of wild flowers.

At a T-junction, take the Path straight ahead on the Dyke: the next stretch is through the grounds of Mellington Hall **17**. You approach through farmland and then enter woods to the west of the mansion, built in 1876 in 'Victorian industrialists' Gothic' style and now a hotel with an extensive caravan park. This is quite near the Dyke but is reasonably screened. Please observe the 'no smoking' request in the woods – and enjoy the seasonal anemones and bluebells. You are at the edge of parkland beyond the house and, after reaching a stream ablaze in spring with marsh marigolds, a swing east takes you on to the Hall drive and then through an arched gateway on to the B4385.

Continue straight ahead on this road for 350 yards (320 metres) with fragmentary Dyke to the east. Cross the Caebitra River, pass a motte on the east **18**, and you reach the A489 junction by the Blue Bell Inn.

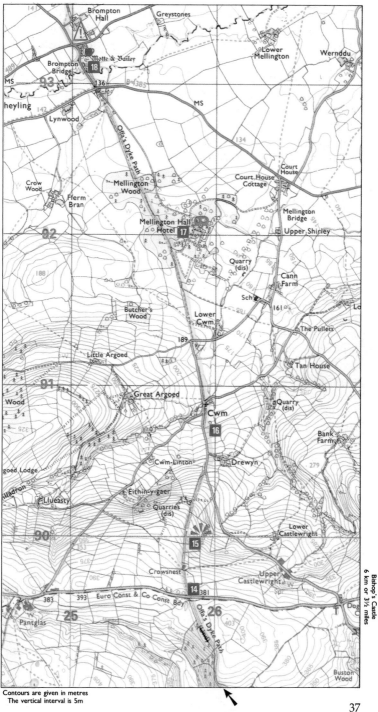

Contours are given in metres
The vertical interval is 5m

Knighton 1

'Tref y Clawdd', the Welsh name, meaning 'town on the Dyke', makes clear Knighton's unique position as the only town where pronounced stretches of Offa's Dyke can be seen in the town itself. These are on the south side of the town crossing Frŷdd Road and then climbing up from the Cwm to follow the line of Offa's Road, and on the west side of the park north of West Street, overlooking the River Teme. The English name means 'town of the horsemen' (the original meaning of 'knight'), again suggesting its strategic significance in the defence of the Marches.

There are two castle sites, both now just mounds, one completely surrounded by buildings among the complicated network of small streets above the town centre; it can just be seen behind the fire station in Market Street. The other, probably earlier site, Bryn y Castell, is in the recreation ground behind the community centre in Bowling Green Lane. From the top there are splendid views up and down the Teme Valley and to the other castle mound.

Knighton is a busy and prosperous market town. While there are few outstanding buildings, there are many interesting ones of different periods. One of the oldest is the medieval cruck-built Old House, hidden away behind the main frontage at the top of Broad Street, near the inevitable clock tower (almost indistinguishable from that at Hay: these must have come 'off the peg'!). From here the narrow High Street rises steeply to the Market Place, with mainly 17th century shops and other small buildings. This old part of town was built on the high ridge leading from and perhaps in the outer bailey of the castle. To the south it falls steeply to the Cwm, where small, haphazardly arranged cottages suggest a more informal settlement. St Edward's Church is on the north side of town: as with so many Border churches, only the tower is medieval, the rest is 1876–97.

The Offa's Dyke Centre 2 in West Street, in the southern corner of the park containing a stretch of Offa's Dyke, is the former primary school. The local Tref y Clawdd Society rescued the building and it has now been converted to a youth hostel (currently (1995) closed awaiting repairs), the Offa's Dyke Association Information Office and an exhibition about King Offa, the Dyke and the Border area generally, and also a library on these topics. The Information Office serves the general visitor to Knighton as well as the specialist Dyke walker and stocks a range of maps, guides and souvenirs.

A number of circular walks from Knighton, exploring the Teme Valley and surrounding hill country, are well documented in a booklet produced by the Offa's Dyke Association. It can be obtained from the Knighton Centre.

Border railways

Knighton is a suitable place to refer to the railways of the Border, since it has a station on the Heart of Wales Line from Shrewsbury to Llanelli and Swansea, which has remained open against all the odds. The line was built in sections by four different companies between 1857 and 1868, passing through magnificent but sparsely populated country. A survey we did as long ago as 1969 showed that for many people without cars in isolated settlements it is the only real link with 'civilisation'. Buses, on the steep and winding roads, take an unconscionable time for any but short journeys. Recent developments, through the active Heart of Wales Line Travellers' Association, have also demonstrated how a railway can encourage tourism. The Knighton station is now only a 'halt' but the elaborate 1861 Gothic-style building survives.

While this line survived the 'Beeching closures' of the 1960s, others serving the Border disappeared then or even earlier. Monmouth, once served by four lines, is now railway-less as are Hay-on-Wye, Kington, Oswestry and Llangollen – apart from a stretch of preserved line and steam trains and exhibits: a 'must' for the enthusiast. The other preserved line near the Path, this time narrow-gauge, is the delightful one from Welshpool to Llanfair Caereinion. Welshpool also has a British Rail line, which you cross at nearby Buttington. Other operational railways serving the Path are at Chepstow, Abergavenny, Chirk and Prestatyn.

The Welsh Border had networks of early horse-drawn tramways and of small industrial railway lines. These are mentioned in the text where remains are visible (e.g. north of Llanymynech). This whole topic is of endless fascination to the railway enthusiast.

Looking south towards Knighton from the Dyke on Panpunton Hill.

41

2 Brompton Crossroads to Buttington Bridge

route passes near to Montgomery and Forden
12¼ miles (20 km)

This section of the route takes the walker over a flat stretch, the valleys of the Caebitra and Camlad, surrounded by hills: Kerry Hill ridge to the south and Town Hill, Montgomery to the west. The dolerite cone of Corndon dominates the view to the east and Long Mountain that to the north. The last of these is climbed by the Path before it drops down to the Severn Valley at Buttington. The Dyke is prominent in all but the Long Mountain stretch and you can speculate on its defensibility over the miles of flat terrain it crosses.

From the A489 crossroads at the Blue Bell, continue north on the Montgomery road for 140 yards. Then take the Brompton Hall drive and, before the house, cross a stile to follow a clear path on the west of the Dyke. Continue along this for over a mile, passing on the way the significantly named Ditches Farm, until you reach and cross the drive to Gwarthlow, the farm you will see above you and to the east. The Path is always on the west of the Dyke except for a short stretch where you are actually walking on it.

Continue to walk in a straight line. Flat farmland it may be but the distant views from here **19**, especially of Corndon Hill and the Kerry Hill ridge, are memorable because these prominent shapes are to be seen from considerable distances to both north and south on the route. The Dyke is of variable height in this sector, reflecting the extent of farming ravages, not its uneven construction: at its best it is still quite an obstacle.

Three fields after the Gwarthlow turn, you approach a patch of woodland, cross a cattle grid on a drive and continue northwards with Dyke and woods now to your west. This is Lymore Park, a classically laid out estate, but the 17th century mansion was demolished in the 1930s. The woods are well stocked with pheasants and partridges and you are also likely to see ducks. At the end of the wood (see map on page 45), the Path crosses a stile to return to the west side of the Dyke and then, after a short stretch on the earthwork, it reaches the B4386 a mile east of Montgomery (see page 52), whose church, castle and hill have dominated the western skyline for some time **20**. This road is on the Montgomery to Shrewsbury bus route.

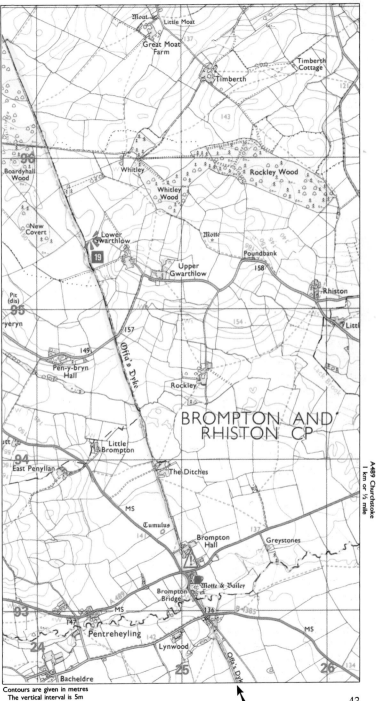

Contours are given in metres
The vertical interval is 5m

Take the path opposite across the road. It is shown as a bridleway but stiles are soon encountered. The Dyke is clear again west of Rownal Covert and that is where you cross it. Go forward to the Rownal Farm drive.

Just before the farm, cross a stile and walk down the east side of a field with the Dyke a prominent feature in the field to your west. A gate leads to a muddy lane past two ruined houses and a second gate leads to a large open field with the River Camlad ahead. The Path used to swing west here to reach and cross the river at Salt Bridge on the B4388, but the route changed in 1985 and now continues north along the Dyke line, using a foot-bridge put up by 'Powys Task Force 07: Knighton 1985'. This is a major improvement to the route, but the former one should not be disregarded by the walker as it is still a useful access point to the Path.

Beyond the Camlad the Path, on the line of the Dyke, soon follows a drive past Pound House to cross a minor road which leads off the B4388.

The Dyke east of Montgomery.

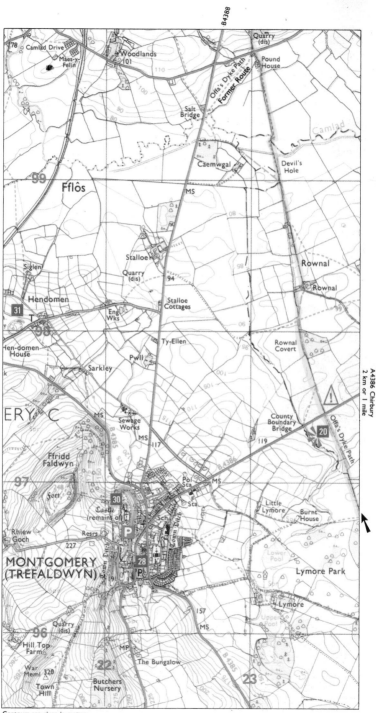

Contours are given in metres
The vertical interval is 5m

You climb a steep bank ahead, thus proving that the Camlad Valley is being left behind, and follow the Dyke at first to its west but then on its eastern side, through a series of fields. After crossing a drive, you reach a small road and follow this west to the B4388. You have no option but to continue north on the B road for about half a mile to the junction with the A490. The Dyke continues in the fields just to the east, and a fine castle mound lies just beyond, but there is no path. A few yards east on the A490 you rejoin the Dyke by passing down the side of a small cottage. Before doing this, however, you may well wish to go north on the A490 for about 300 yards to use the facilities of Forden (Cock Hotel and limited shop in garage beyond it).

The route continues beside the Dyke across a series of small fields just east of the houses of Forden: a sort of 'end of the gardens' walk. This leads to a small road coming out of the village and continuing directly ahead and very steeply uphill. Going south, this is the best point from which to divert to the amenities of Forden. As you climb, reflect that you are following the course of a Roman road, which continues along Long Mountain, *and* walking on the line of the Dyke; at first it is the high bank forming the eastern edge of the road and then the western one **21**. Near the top the road swings and your way is through the gateway ahead into the Leighton Estate (see page 52). Pass below the Victorian Greenwood Lodge and climb the broad grassy track that lies ahead among trees.

Continue forward in Leighton Woods after joining a larger drive at the top of the first drive, by a group of monkey puzzle trees **22**. There are views steeply down to the west with Leighton Hall and the Severn Valley beyond. When the drive starts to drop, turn uphill on a smaller track which is often muddy from forestry work, and in 100 yards take a footpath left (west) to cross the Dyke (which has never been far from your route). Then swing immediately right (north), with the Dyke now high on your right (east), through young plantations. Care in following the correct route is important hereabouts **A**. Shortly afterwards there is a steep descent to a junction with a driveway which you follow east at first, but which then reaches and doubles back round the east end of 'Offa's Pool', the storage part of the estate water works **23**. On reaching a second pond take the smaller path on its east side, which climbs through trees to leave the estate at a small road. If you are lucky enough to walk this stretch in February, you will be rewarded on this last path by a carpet of tens of thousands of snowdrops **24**.

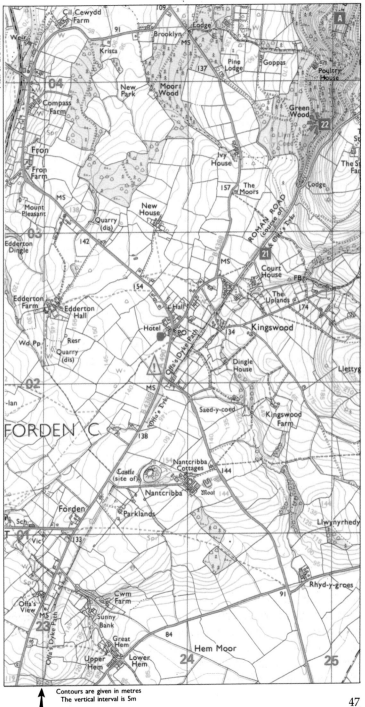

Welshpool (Trallwng)
4 km or 2½ miles

Contours are given in metres
The vertical interval is 5m

47

Climb westwards for 100 yards on this road and then, at the top of the rise, swing sharply east along a surfaced track, still climbing. Where this divides, cross a stile between the two branches and go up the side of a field, soon with a wood (Phillips's Gorse) on the left (north). Just before the top of the wood a stile takes you north-east along its edge and then up field edges to the top of Beacon Ring hill fort **25**. As you climb, the views to the west over Welshpool and the Severn Valley open out and the mass of the volcanic Breidden Hills is now also seen to the north **26**, as you circle the west side of the high single bank of the Iron Age fortification. The middle of the fort is thickly planted and a plaque at the south end dates the trees to 1953. The fort is at the west end, and highest point (1,338 feet/ 408 metres), of the Long Mountain range that has closed off the view for northbound walkers from the Path on the Montgomery Plain. Forden was 900 feet (275 metres) lower.

Buttington, 2½ miles (4 km) ahead, is over 1,000 feet (300 metres) below the fort. The route is mainly through farmland and needs to be followed closely **B**. Going south, of course, the climb is the problem **C**: take it slowly and admire the views to the north and west. Northbound walkers leave Beacon Ring opposite the point where they reached it, just west of a television booster station. Walk at the edge of a plantation and then turn into the fir woods on a forestry track. After about 150 yards a narrow path right (north) takes you out of the woods to the edge of a large field. Swing north-west, diagonally over this field, avoiding the top of a cwm rising from the west. (For southbound walkers the wood is seen across the field and the entry is a stile at about its middle point.) At the furthest corner of the field there is a stile and the way is now all downhill with Buttington, your objective, clearly visible.

Descend three fields steeply to reach a stile and gate at the bottom right (north) corner which leads to a farm lane. Go 150 yards along this and then, when it swings, turn north-west under an arch of ivy and over a stile to descend through more fields to a minor road. Go *south-west* on the road for a short distance and then, at a stile, resume the steep descent northwards. Pass in front of a small cottage and then down its approach lane towards the large Stone House Farm. Reach the corner of a farm building and continue forward, keeping the house well above you, to reach its drive. Where this swings through a gateway, your way bears left (north-west) down fields beside a small stream. Eventually a stone footbridge

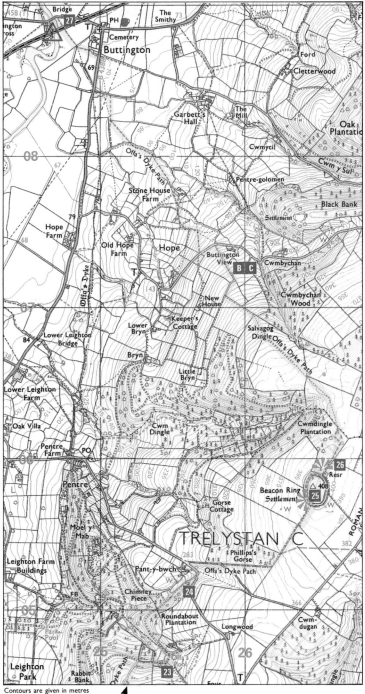

crosses the stream. Now your route is simply diagonally across two fields and along a short stretch of lane to the B4388, by the new 'Offa's Dyke' Business Park, a little south of the church and the Green Dragon Inn.

When rejoined the Dyke is only a slight bank above the B4388. Turn north on the B road for 200 yards but *before* the Green Dragon go through a gate by some houses. Cross two fields and footbridges, then swing to cross (*with care*) the Shrewsbury to Welshpool railway and reach the A458 at the east end of Buttington Bridge over the Severn **27**. If you want to visit Welshpool and Powis Castle, see page 64.

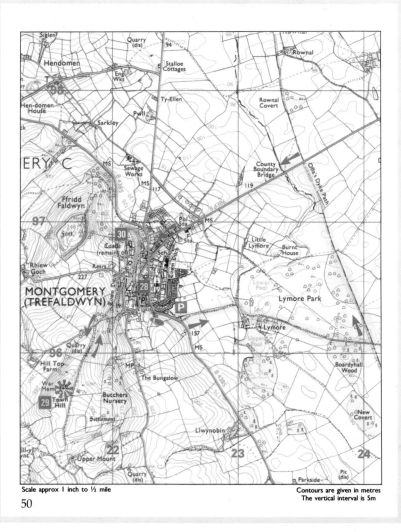

Scale approx 1 inch to ½ mile

Contours are given in metres
The vertical interval is 5m

A CIRCULAR WALK FROM MONTGOMERY

3¾ miles (6 km)

There is car parking (grid ref. 224 963) on the south side of Montgomery off the B4385, beside the recreation ground. Follow the road south to the wicket gate (signposted to Offa's Dyke) to the east. Take the track from the gate, via two further wicket gates, to join the Lymore Park estate road; continue past the cricket ground. Crossing a cattle grid, the road passes through Boardyhall Wood plantation to reach the Path at a breach in Offa's Dyke, which here marks the England–Wales border. Pass through to the east side and follow the earthwork north. After the third stile the route reverts to the west side, though by a deft switching of the border the Path remains in England. Where the hedge ceases, the Dyke becomes a major ditch and bank feature, coinciding with the scarp overlooking the stream that flows from Lymore Park's Lower Pool.

Joining the Chirbury road (B4386) at the gate, leave the Path and Dyke on course for the Camlad, but instead head south-west on the road directly back to Montgomery – in the process re-entering Wales at County Boundary Bridge. At the road junction turn left along Princes Street, to enter Broad Street **28** right at the heart of Montgomery. Follow the steepening road up between the Town Hall and the Dragon Hotel, passing the old county gaol. Upon reaching the minor road, cross over to the kissing gate and ascend the path above the Town Ditch.

Joining the farm track, ascend to a gate, with progressively broader views to the ancient hills of south Shropshire, and leave the track half right (south-west), and go up the pasture to the summit of Bryn y Dref (Town Hill) **29**. The noble pillar is a memorial to the brave men of Montgomeryshire who gave their lives in the two World Wars. There is also an Automobile Association toposcope, giving a cursory appraisal of the panorama. Backtracking to the kissing gate, go half left through the castle car park and along the path, crossing two wooden bridges to inspect Montgomery Castle **30**, impressively perched upon a high crag above the town (see page 52). Then take the path descending half left (south) from near the first castle bridge, down to a kissing gate into Arthur Street. Conclude the walk by turning right, and prior to leaving the town centre southwards via Broad Street make a point of visiting the Old Bell, home of the Montgomery Civic Society whose exhibition is open all week in summer and on winter weekends.

Montgomery (Trefaldwyn)

This delightful small town **28** is overlooked by castle ruins on a spectacular rocky site. The castle **30**, a row of wards (fortified courtyards) set along a ridge, was begun in 1223, with alterations and additions over the next 400 years. The outer defence was a circuit of walls and ditches which also enclosed the town, and traces of which survive. This castle's predecessor was founded by the powerful Norman lord, Roger de Montgomery, about 1070. He had a good geographical-cum-strategic reason for choosing this site for his fortified town. Wales was the prize, and controlling access was the key to it. With the River Severn forming a corridor right into the heart of central Wales, the ford Rhydwhyman was the strategically crucial point to dominate. Ffridd Faldwyn was the Iron Age control point, Forden Gaer the Roman fort, and Hen Domen (a motte and bailey castle north of the town) the first Norman defensive site **31** (see map on page 45). Birmingham University has excavated at the latter annually since 1960. Exeter University has now taken on this work.

The Welsh name of the town (Trefaldwyn) refers to a later Norman owner, Baldwin. The town itself, founded in 1227, has one of the best preserved examples of a medieval planned street layout. During a period of prosperity many of the buildings acquired smart 18th century Georgian façades, particularly along Broad Street (which lives up to its name, being almost a town square), and terminating in the fine town hall. The large St Nicholas's Church was probably started at the same time as the major castle, but has fine internal roofs and other woodwork dating from around 1500. (We recall a vigorous discussion between two eminent historians, in the church, on whether this churchyard might have been the site of the first Montgomery castle.) Much of the town's importance was later lost to Welshpool and Newtown, which proved to be more accessible for canal and railway communications. The town has an active civic society which has, with understandable civic pride, gone to some pains to give visitors a feast of information about their historic town, including plaques on relevant buildings.

Leighton Estate

Most of what you see dates from the time of John Naylor, a Liverpool banker, who took possession of the estate in 1849. He built a great 'Gothic' mansion and a new parish church, with a

Montgomery Castle, the earliest parts of which date from the 13th century.

spire visible from miles around, both by the architect W. H. Gee. The house had elaborate gardens and plantations on the adjoining slopes, including a redwood grove (now owned and managed by the Royal Forestry Society), wellingtonias and 'monkey puzzles' **22**, many of which you will pass on the Path through the estate.

Particularly remarkable were the pioneer farming improvements, including elaborate model buildings, many lit by gas from works on the estate, and a complex system of water engineering. 'Offa's Pool' **23** and the other pond you pass in the woods formed part of the collecting system. This drove a turbine for power-driven farm equipment and also produced liquid manure from bonemeal and guano to fertilise, as well as irrigate, the fields below. The remains of the great tank where this took place and the terminal of a funicular railway can still be seen on top of Moel y Mab, a knoll to the west of the point where the Path turns east to Beacon Ring.

The Georgian square and Town Hall at Montgomery.

3 Buttington Bridge to Llanymynech

via Pool Quay Lock and Four Crosses
10½ miles (17 km)

'The dull bit' is a common, but unfair, description of the stretch of Path between Buttington and Llanymynech. You walk by the Severn with the Breidden Hills across the river for company, complete a section on a restored canal towpath and follow some sections of the Dyke. Flat, it is true, but there is much to enjoy in this interlude between the hills – and these are never far away.

Cross Buttington Bridge westwards on the A458 and turn north on the first farm drive, to Talybont. A little further along the main road is the turning up to Buttington Wharf **32** on the Montgomery Canal, a branch of the Shropshire Union Canal, which provides an alternative route (see map opposite). From the junction of the A458 and the A483, there are buses to Oswestry, Shrewsbury and Welshpool. Pass between Talybont Farm and outbuildings to the Severn bank and follow this, and two flood embankments (*not* the Dyke) which cut off meanders, until in three-quarters of a mile river, embankment and A483 come together. The views south to Buttington Bridge and across the river to the Breiddens are splendid on this stretch **33**. Cross the road with care and walk along the verge for 250 yards until the Montgomery Canal **34** is beside the road at the top of a rise.

Join the well-cared-for canal towpath and continue north on this for 1¼ miles (2 km) as far as Pool Quay Lock. You soon pass a fine restored swing bridge over the canal **35**. This carries a track to Abbey Barn, the only visible structure to remind you of the 12th century Cistercian abbey of Strata Marcella **36**. This lay in the fields below the canal and road but, like Grace Dieu on the Path north of Monmouth, there are no visible remains. The Path continues on the towpath for a further ¾ mile (1.2 km) to just before the attractive Pool Quay lock and the 1820s lock-keeper's cottage. It then slopes down to the busy A483 and you have to walk 200 yards north on this before the fingerpost shows the muddy field path sloping down to the River Severn **A**. The Powis Arms at Pool Quay is on the main road just south of the Path; the post office is closed. (As an 'alternative' to the River Severn stretch, the towpath can be followed to Four Crosses – see page 60.)

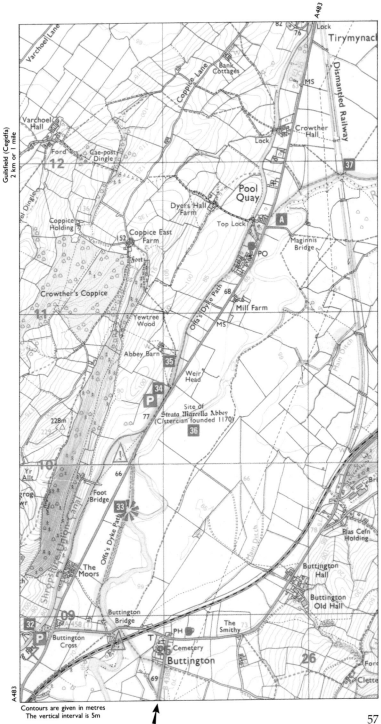

Gulisfield (Cegidfa)
2 km or 1 mile

A483

Contours are given in metres
The vertical interval is 5m

57

The Path reaches the river just south of a bridge over a tributary stream. Once over this the way is clear on a series of flood defence embankments raised above the river and cutting off most of the meanders. For the first 2¾ miles (4.5 km) the only individual landmark is the track of the former Cambrian Railway main line from Oswestry to Newtown which you cross near its start. The bridge abutments **37** remain as gaunt memorials to a mode of transport that superseded the canal but has now gone, though the waterway has been restored. This is a favoured fishing stretch of the river – look out for kingfishers – and swans are also happy here. The Breidden Hills and the Criggion radio masts dominate the view across the river, with Long Mountain prominent to the south. After this first stretch there is, for a short time, a road below the embankment and the hamlet of Rhyd-esgyn: the gardens are especially colourful in spring and in a couple of cases they slope up the embankment just below you.

The river soon swings east. You continue on the embankment to cross a sluice gate and swing sharp west on the bank of the drainage channel of the New Cut. Three hundred yards after the bend, cross the channel by the farm track over Derwas Bridge into a large field and go across it diagonally. Should you be walking at a time of heavy floods, you might find this field under water **B**, in which case you would have to make a long detour west along the New Cut embankment to the nearest road. This is unlikely, however, and you will probably find the plank footbridge that takes you over a tributary stream quite easily, and cross a stile on to another embankment. This flood defence work is on the line of Offa's Dyke, which probably forms its foundation. Where the embankment turns west you continue on a hedged path to reach a small road by The Nea farmhouse: go east and immediately north again, over a stile and go anti-clockwise round a small field, to gain a further embankment (see top end of map on page 59).

You are now on an embankment which is very like the Dyke and this is followed north-north-west from here to the B4393 Rhos road. You continue across a further series of fields along the Dyke to reach the west edge of the farmyard of Gornel. Cross this, keeping as far away from the house as you can, and gathering as little mud as possible **C**. Pass a small sewage works and then a wicket gate and you are on the platform of the former Four Crosses Station of the Cambrian Railway, now a factory. Make your way carefully out through the station yard to cross

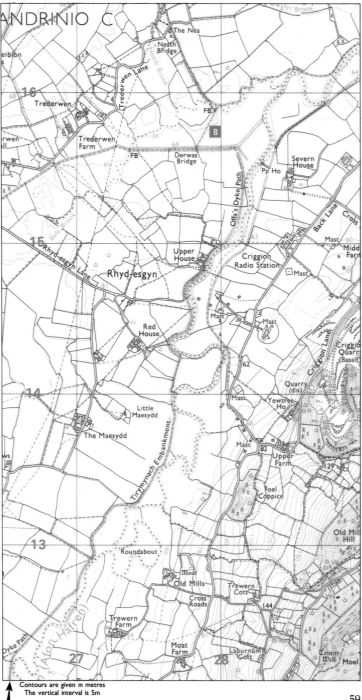

Contours are given in metres
The vertical interval is 5m

the other branch of the B4393. The village shop is to the west but the Path crosses a grassy triangle straight ahead, with a fine stretch of Dyke across it and a pool in the ditch.

When the Path was first opened the route north from Four Crosses ran along the busy A483 all the way into Llanymynech. With the canal restored a wiser route was possible and now you follow the road for only a short distance, and this has a pavement. Note the Dyke over the hedge on the east and the fine ironwork on the Golden Lion. Turn west on Parson's Lane and reach the canal towpath at Pont-y-Person Farm. In three-quarters of a mile you pass above the ruins of the burnt-out Pentreheylin Hall and then cross the fine stone aqueduct over the River Vyrnwy **38**. An almost equally good road bridge provides an immediate view west, and beyond you can see the Berwyn Mountains on even a half decent day. It is fine territory for the pair of swans that are often ready to greet you here. A little way on are the restored Carreghofa Locks **39** with the tollhouse marking the junction of the separate ownerships of the Ellesmere and Montgomery Canals. The restored site was opened in November 1987 by Baroness White of Rhymney, who for many years has been involved with conservation work in Wales. It will be one of the showplaces on the canal when it is fully passable again: some road realignment will be necessary, as you will have observed. Past a further swan site and you are soon crossing under the A483 at Llanymynech. Climb a flight of steps on the south side and continue north over the stretch of canal on which you have just walked. The shops and amenities of the village are just to your south.

The Breiddens

These hills are an outstanding feature of the view for many miles, particularly from the Severn embankments. Formed of hard igneous rocks, they rise steeply from the surrounding plain. Unfortunately they are being heavily quarried for road stone. At a prominent summit at 1,200 feet (365 metres) is Admiral Rodney's Pillar, erected in 1781 to commemorate his naval victory in the French Wars. There are remains of an Iron Age hill fort and evidence of both earlier and later settlement. As there is no suitable bridge over the Severn, no short circuits including these hills are included in this book: the best access would be from the Shrewsbury road east of Buttington.

A483

Carreghofa
Farm 21
Mount
Dismantled Railway
Sch
Walls
Bridge
PO
Llanymynech
FB
Sch 76
Aqueduct
MS
St Benion's
Well
Causeway Lane
Pont
Llanymynech
IOFA C Wern
Carreghofa
Locks 39
awdd
coch
Former Route
Offa's Dyke Path
Afon Efyrnwy
69
Pentref
20
65
64
Afon Efyrnwy (River Vyrnwy)
65
Former Route
Offa's Dyke Path
Rhandregynwen
Aqueduct
Bridge
nwy
65
Afon E
Aqueduct
38
Ty Coch Farm
66
Pentreheylin
Hall
66
FB
Llandysilio
19
B 4393
77
Parson's Lane
Oak
Coppice
MS
LLAND
Bryn-mawr
Farm
Pont-y-
Person
Sch
Oldfield
Gwerglodd-
beillied
Courthouse Lane
Four
Crosses
69
Wks
Frondeg
Llys Rhysnant
Canal Road
PO
The City
106
Rhysnant
Farm
Dismantled Railway
Sarn-wen
18
Welshpool
Road
C Gornel
Rhysnant-
fach
The Fields
Rhysnant
Hall
Domen
Wood
Ffynnon
-Cap-Cesh
Rhos
Farm
Earthwork
Shaft
(dis)
School Brook
Bridge
MS Little
Penthryn
70
Offa's Dyke
80
Penthryn-fawr
B 4393
A
17
26
Penthryn
Farm
Towing Path
Maerdy
Farm
Rhos
Royal
27
71
Maerdy La

Looking south from Llanymynech Hill to the Breiddens.

63

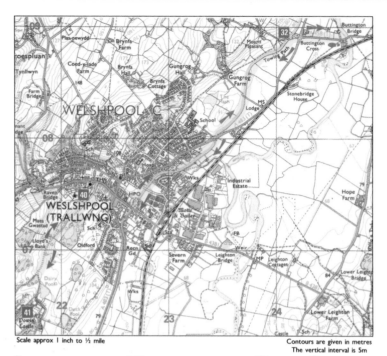

Scale approx 1 inch to ½ mile

Contours are given in metres
The vertical interval is 5m

SPUR ROUTE TO WELSHPOOL AND POWIS CASTLE

3 miles (5 km) each way

Walkers arriving at Buttington Bridge (River Severn) may relish the opportunity of a break from their Offan progression by strolling south-west via Welshpool (Y Trallwng) to visit Powis Castle, one of the premier National Trust properties in Wales.

Advance from the Path along the A458 to the junction with the A483, and go directly across the new, busy roundabout to reach Buttington Wharf car park and picnic site **32** (grid ref. 242 089). Consult the signboards to learn something of the history of this stretch of the Montgomery Canal (and see page 66), specifically the lime burning carried out here in the early 19th century. The lime was used to improve the fertility of the pastures on Long Mountain and the Breidden Hills.

Walk south along the towpath into Welshpool **40** (see page 65). Leave the canal at Welshpool Wharf to go into the town centre, continuing west along the High Street. Pass the Town Hall, and turn left opposite Doaxe's Passage into the short approach road (car parking) to Powis Castle outer park gateway (pedestrian access to the castle and grounds **41** (see page 65)). Retrace your steps, to continue along Offa's Dyke Path.

Welshpool (Y Trallwng) **40**

This is a busy agricultural and industrial town, particularly noted for its large cattle market (held on Mondays). The church of St Mary dates from 1250 but has been much changed. There are buildings of many periods and, by the canal, the Powysland and Montgomeryshire Canal Museum, with collections which include finds from Strata Marcella Abbey, near the Path.

Over three-quarters of a mile (1 km) south-west of the town, on a commanding rock outcrop, is the magnificent Powis Castle (Y Castell Coch – the Red Castle, from the colour of the sandstone from which it is built) **41**. This was the stronghold of the Princes of Powys and has a complex history, the owners being sometimes on the Welsh and sometimes on the English side in successive Border conflicts. The earliest buildings date from about 1200, but the castle is not a ruin: the interior was converted to a grand country house from the time of its acquisition by the Herbert family in 1587. Later the house became the seat of the Clive family, and there is now a Clive Museum. The fine gardens, terraced down the slope, are also of great interest and historical importance. Powis Castle is owned by the National Trust and hours of opening should be checked.

The north-east façade of Powis Castle.

CIRCULAR ROUTE USING THE MONTGOMERY CANAL

12 miles (19 km)

The Severnside portion of the Path north from Pool Quay to Four Crosses can be integrated into an entertaining circular waterside walk by following the Montgomery Canal towpath northwards from Pool Quay Lock, and returning on the Path, or vice versa.

The Montgomery Canal 34

The towpath of this canal – a branch of the Shropshire Union Canal – forms part of two short sections of the Path, south of Pool Quay and north of Four Crosses. The whole of it can be used as an alternative route from Buttington (from the wharf) to Llanymynech and, with the Path, it forms the basis of a range of options for circular walks (see above and page 57). The canal itself, one of the products of the 1790s canal boom, was part of a scheme to link the Severn Valley, as far west as Newtown, with the Dee and Mersey. The railways killed it, and it became so derelict and overgrown that as late as the 1960s a party of pioneering Offa's Dyke walkers near Pool Quay felt themselves to be in danger from a group of frisky pigs on the other side who seemed ready to charge across the muddy reed beds.

This is no longer the case. British Waterways, in co-operation with the Prince of Wales's Committee, the EEC, local councils and naturalists' trusts, are engaged in major restoration projects that will provide a range of water leisure uses and a secure haven for wildlife. Locks are being restored, the towpath made safe, information boards and an exhibition centre, at Welshpool, provided. One particularly pleasing development is the conversion of a narrow boat, the *Heulwen Sunshine*, for use by the disabled. The whole of this 35-mile (56-km) project will take several years to complete and visitors wanting information on the amenities available at any time should consult British Waterways' Leisure Officer, Canal Wharf, Llanymynech, Powys (tel. Llanymynech (01691) 831237). The restoration of the through route, where this has been blocked by 'improvements' in the roads crossing the canal, will be a major task.

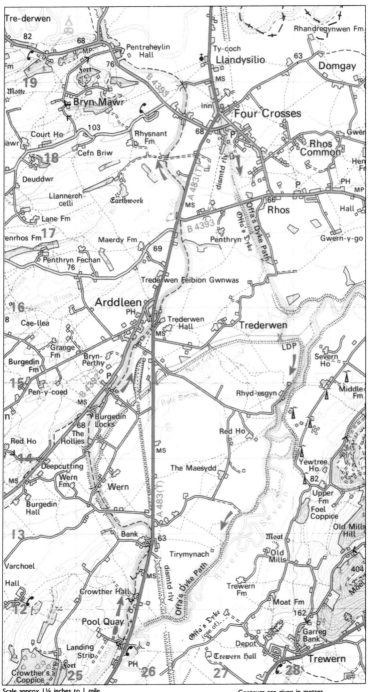

Tre-derwen

Rhandregynwen Fm

82 68 MP
Pentreheylin Hall

Ty-coch
Llandysilio 63 Domgay

Fm 76

19 Fort B 4393 (T) Inn MS

Motte Bryn Mawr Four Crosses

Court Ho 103 Rhysnant Fm 68 P Rhos Common

18 Cefn Briw Gwern

Deuddwr Hen
PH MP

Llannerch-celli Earthwork 66 Rhos

Lane Fm MS Penthryn Dyke Hall

enrhos Fm 17 Maerdy Fm 69 Penthryn Dyke Gwern-y-go

Penthryn Fechan 76

Trederwen Feibion Gwnwas

16 Maerdy Brook Arddleen LDP
Cae-llea PH Trederwen Hall Trederwen Severn Ho

Grange Fm MS Middle Fm

Burgedin Fm Bryn-Perthy Rhyd-esgyn

15 Pen-y-coed MS B 4393 Red Ho Yewtree Ho 82

Burgedin Locks Red Ho Upper Fm

Red Ho The Hollies MS Foel Coppice

14 Deepcutting The Maesydd Old Mills Hill

MS Wern Fm Wern Moat Old Mills

Burgedin Hall A 483 (T) River Severn 404

13 Bank 63 Moat

Varchoel Tirymynach Trewern Fm Moat Fm 162

Hall Crowther Hall Trewern Garreg Bank

12 Pool Quay Offa's Dyke Depot Trewern

Landing Strip Offa's Dyke (site of) Trewern Hall 28

Crowther's Fort 25 26 PH 27
Coppice

Scale approx 1¼ inches to 1 mile

Contours are given in metres
The vertical interval is 10m

67

4 Llanymynech to Chirk Mill

via Porth-y-waen and Trefonen
14 miles (22.5 km)

This section of the route covers the former mining areas round Llanymynech and Nantmawr, the spectacular views from Moelydd, the former Oswestry racecourse, and ends with superb stretches of Dyke towards Chirk Castle grounds.

The route up to the golf course on top of Llanymynech Hill has to be followed with care. Start northwards on the A483 but after 200 yards fork on to a minor road. Climb through a rock cutting and, in 400 yards, turn east opposite a letter box, up past cottages, and on to a path ahead. At a junction your way turns left (north) and is very steep. At the next junction turn westwards and pass below old quarries (do *not* go into them) and kilns, and then gradually swing north under the prominent shoulder of Asterley Rocks to reach the golf course by the 14th tee. The course is noted for the extensive views westwards to the Berwyn Mountains **42**.

The course of the Dyke itself up to the golf course is uncertain, but once there it lies at the western edge of the course and hilltop, and your way is by and just to the east of it, passing below the edge of the 14th tee **A** and then turning north. To preserve walker-golfer relations it is important not to stray from the Path on to the fairways; the Dyke itself is the guide.

After over half a mile, you reach a steep gully and the Path descends it westwards very steeply **B** through trees (the Dyke continues along the hill edge). At the bottom swing north across two fields and down a minor road. Where the road turns east, continue down fields to cross a mineral railway, the Tanat Valley line **43** (see page 78). After two more fields and a drive, you reach the A495 at Porth-y-waen.

The remains of the Dyke are lost in mines and quarries to the east of the route and you do not meet it again until north of Trefonen. The Path crosses the main A495 diagonally, goes west across a field, and soon turns north up a path between houses to emerge on a suburban road. Turn west on this for three-quarters of a mile. You soon leave the houses behind, and beyond an old mineral railway the route is pleasant enough along this small lane. Opposite the extensive Cefn Farm on the south side of the road, descend a large field and go through a belt of firs to reach a small road just west of the mining village of Nantmawr.

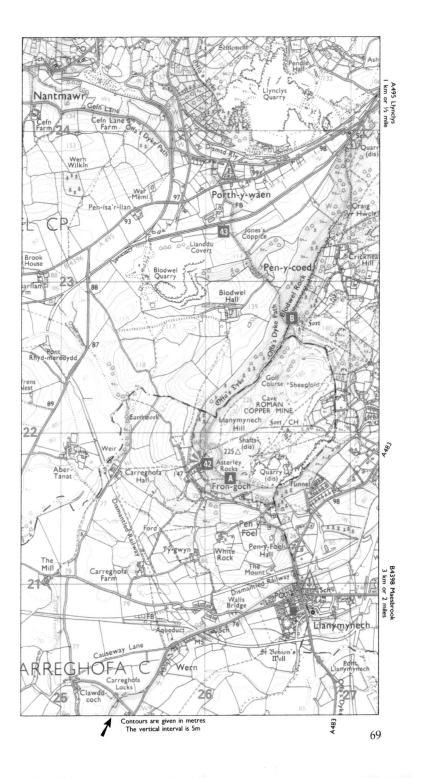

Turn east to pass among its houses and chapels and, just before the phone box, go north up some steps and then up a path between houses. After a very steep climb up two fields you reach another small road which you follow west, soon taking the north way at a fork. Before the second house a path slopes steeply up into woods: this is Jones's Rough **44**, the southern slope of Moelydd Hill, and now a reserve of the Shropshire Trust for Nature Conservation. This 8-acre (3.2-hectare) limestone scree site has yew, hazel, spruce and larch, as well as orchids and stinking hellebore. The Path has been improved with steps. At the top of the wood, continue forward and swing left (north-west) above a restored cottage before swinging right (north-east) to the top of Moelydd. This, at 934 feet (285 metres), is one of the most extensive viewpoints on the whole Path **45**. From the memorial flagpole, which marks a coming of age, the Berwyns and even the Arans can be seen to the west. As a contrast, to the north-east the Delamere and Peckforton Hills are visible over the flat land of north Shropshire, and to the south the view extends to the Long Mynd and Church Stretton Hills – 30 miles in every direction but north. To resume the route from Moelydd summit you have to make a three-quarter turn **C** and then descend a small ridge south-east before picking up an easterly track. In a few yards you cross a stile leading towards Moelydd Uchaf Farm.

Before reaching the farm, swing east to join a north-south lane. This is a pleasant track which passes a rock outcrop and, through the yard of Ty-Canol Farm, reaches a road. Almost opposite, a field path leads north-east past two prominent trees and over a footbridge to the houses of Trefonen village. The Path turns north just before the village centre (but by continuing forward you soon reach the two inns, shop and post office, and the bus route to Oswestry).

The Path continues north by a small road and then bears right on a footpath below gardens; the Dyke can be seen to the east. Cross a small road and slant up and east to follow a fine high stretch of Dyke. A little way up a stile takes you from its west to its east side **D** and then you walk on the earthwork to reach a road junction at the top of the hill by Pentre-shannel Farm. Cross the road and go steeply down the road ahead to the Morda Valley and a former mill, now restored as an inn.

Turn east at the inn and immediately north again at a cottage by a subsidiary stream. Soon you begin to climb steeply up Candy Woods. Near the top, swing south-east and immediately

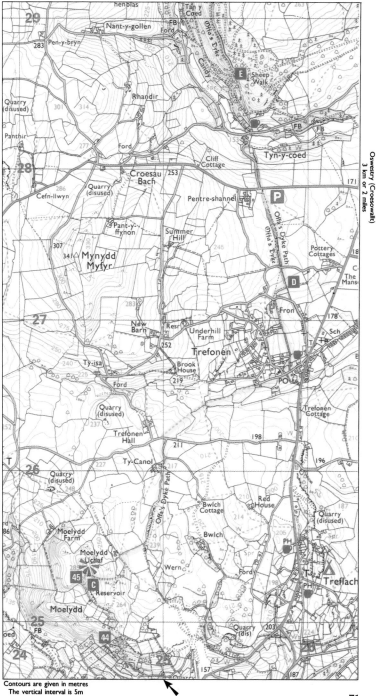

Contours are given in metres
The vertical interval is 5m

71

north again **E**, with the Dyke just above you. The next mile is glorious **46**, especially in spring for the flowers and in autumn for the colours. To the west there is a steep drop through woods, and to the north the Dyke is clearly outlined on Baker's Hill ahead. You pass curious rock outcrops and a seat in a grotto formed from one of them. After about a mile on the ridge, go through a gate to the east at a path junction **F** and then immediately north through a little dell. The Dyke is now to your west. Stiles lead to broad tracks going north over the remains of Oswestry Racecourse. Part of the track is still visible and some of the scattered cottages and the remains of the grandstand, which now has a toposcope, date from its heyday in the early 18th to mid-19th centuries. Just to the east is a picnic site **47** with car park, toilets and a second toposcope showing the panorama from the top, at 971 feet (296 metres). From here the B4580 goes east to Oswestry 2 miles (3.2 km) away.

The next mile ought to be along the fine section of Dyke on Baker's Hill but there is no right of way here and the Path follows the minor road to its east, directly north from the junction between the racetrack and the B4580, to Carreg-y-big Farm, built right on the Dyke. Note the splendid view of the Dyke to the south **48**, then cross a stile just north of the farm to begin climbing on the English side of a fine stretch of Dyke, with a particularly well-marked ditch. The view east, to the plain of

A stretch of the Dyke above Carreg-y-big.

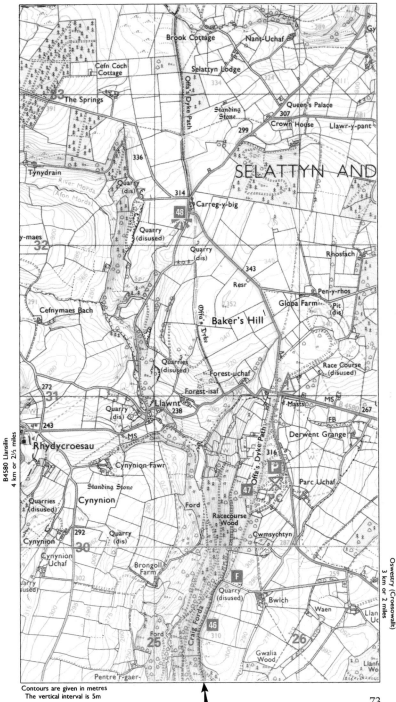

Contours are given in metres
The vertical interval is 5m

73

north Shropshire, is very wide. Pass the east edge of a wood, cross a dingle, and Orseddwen farm is just ahead. The Path leaves the Dyke by the farm drive, and in a few yards turns north to follow a wide track one field to its east, and climbs the shoulder of Selattyn Hill. Reach the corner of a wood at the top of the slope, turn west over the ridge top and soon turn north to enter the top of a green lane with the Dyke just to the west. The descent gets steeper as you join the drive from Woodside, a cottage with a marvellous garden actually on the Dyke. The earthwork is prominent ahead of you, rising on the slope above the next east–west valley of Morlas Brook.

The drive reaches the B4579 at Craignant, well to the east of the Dyke, but the point where the road crosses the Dyke is marked by a large 19th century stone **49** built into a high crenellated stone wall: well worth a short diversion past a roadside picnic site. The return of the Path to the Dyke from the B road is a little complex **G**. Go a few yards east and take the tiny road dropping to the brook; swing east past old kilns and then north-west past a farmhouse. The road ends here and continues as a green lane rising to a small road. Go west on this for 100 yards/metres to reach the Dyke. Turn north to follow its east side up a series of fields.

Beyond a small road, continue on the east side of the Dyke and at once you are greeted by the view ahead to Chirk Castle **50**. The next obstacle is the deep ravine of Nanteris, 'Dirty Dingle' in the lore of Dyke walkers **H**, a term no longer justified since the building of more than 80 steps and a fine footbridge by Ian Rowat (then the Offa's Dyke Development Officer), the Royal Engineers and Shropshire County Council in 1986. Now that you no longer have to slither up and down, you can see what a lovely valley this is. The descent to the Ceiriog Valley now starts. Chirk Castle looms ever larger and to the east the viaduct and aqueduct in Chirk are clearly visible. The Path is by the Dyke or on it just here, and the walking is neither comfortable nor routed to minimise erosion **I**. Take a path from the bottom of the last field of the drop and then go left between houses: the one at the corner sports 'Offa's Dyke Path' in mosaic. It is worth diverting 100 yards along the road to the east to see some very fine, well preserved lime kilns. Do take care and do not trespass into the woods behind the kilns. The road ahead soon crosses the Ceiriog, with impressive views both ways **51**, and reaches the B4500 by the Chirk Mill entrance to the castle. This has a bus route, but no public facilities.

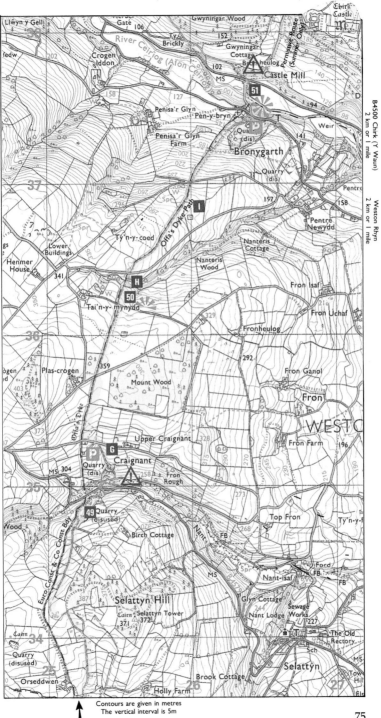

Contours are given in metres
The vertical interval is 5m

A CIRCULAR WALK THROUGH CANDY WOODS

3 miles (5 km) (see map on page 73 and below)

From the Old Racecourse picnic site **47** (grid ref. 259 305) (see page 73) walk south-west to accompany the Offa's Dyke Path through the top of Racecourse Wood, join the Dyke through a breach gate **F**, and continue along it by scenic Craig Forda to reach the Old Mill Inn in the Morda Brook Valley. Refreshed? Then backtrack along the Path into the delightful Candy Woods **46**. Where the Dyke Path turns steeply uphill to join the Dyke itself, continue straight on the contouring path, keeping parallel to and above the brook, towards and beyond Tan-y-coed, then ascend the clear path on the replanted hillside. Near the top cross a stile, with an ingenious dog flap, to regain the gated Dyke breach. Retrace your steps north to visit the remains of the old grandstand, where a viewmarker provided by Oswestry Rotary Club has been sited at the highest point, notable for the view west to the Berwyn Mountains.

In the series *Walks in Shropshire*, Shropshire County Council (Shire Hall, Shrewsbury, SY2 6DN) publishes two descriptive leaflets of short circular walks in the vicinity of Offa's Dyke from the car parks at Craignant and Racecourse Common.

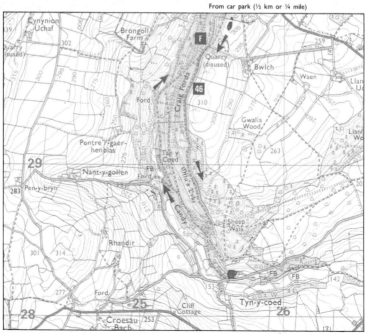

From car park (½ km or ¼ mile)

Contours are given in metres
The vertical interval is 5m

A hedge- and tree-lined section of the Dyke near Pentre-shannel.

Oswestry

Oswestry was one of the great Marcher strongholds. Its castle, the mound of which, with some fragments of masonry, is preserved in a 'town park' setting, was held by the Fitzalan family. The town had the usual turbulent history of a Border centre in the ensuing centuries. It is larger and not as immediately attractive as many Border towns but there are old buildings, most notably the Llwyd Mansion of 1604 and St Oswald's Church, the lower part of whose tower is 13th century. Though in Shropshire, it is a very Welsh town. You will often hear Welsh being spoken by the country people who come in on market days. Oswestry was the centre of the Cambrian railway system, but this has now completely gone.

The early history of Oswestry appears in its name, after St Oswald, King of Northumbria, reputedly slain here in battle against Penda of Mercia in 642; and in two notable monuments in the environs of the town. A mile to the north is Old Oswestry, one of the largest Iron Age hill forts in Britain, its many embankments and ditches standing out strongly when seen in silhouette from the Gobowen road to its east. Later, Wat's Dyke, possibly a precursor of Offa's (see page 15) made use of these embankments in its north–south course. In its own right, Wat's Dyke is seen on either side of the hill fort and it runs through the east side of Oswestry town.

The mining areas of north-west Shropshire and its Powys border

Mineral working north-west of Llanymynech started at a very early date – probably in prehistoric times. The Romans mined copper and silver on Llanymynech Hill, and burial remains and finds of coins and pottery suggest that the miners lived in man-made caves on the slopes of the hill.

Further from Llanymynech, where the land slopes up towards the Berwyns, there lies a sparsely populated area, difficult of access but full of history, with Stone Age megaliths, Bronze Age trackways, Iron Age hill forts and Roman roads, many of which may have mining origins. There are written records of slate working in 1586 and lead mining in 1692; granite and phosphates followed later. Round Porth-y-waen there was, and still is, limestone quarrying.

All this activity increased in the late 18th and 19th centuries, using the newly available means of transport – canals (see pages 66 and 94) and railways with branch and industrial lines in the Cain, Vyrnwy, Tanat and Ceiriog Valleys. The Tanat Valley light railway **43**, from Oswestry to Llangynog, completed in 1904, was a latecomer but survived to 1960. You cross the track near Porth-y-waen and there are many fascinating remains of the railway itself, and the associated mineral working, up the valley to the west.

The villages, such as Llanymynech, Porth-y-waen and Nantmawr, which served the mining industry, are settlements of a quite different character to those associated with the more typical agricultural industry of the Border country.

An old limestone quarry on Llanymynech Hill. Copper and silver were mined here in Roman times.

Old Oswestry, one of the most striking hill forts of the Welsh Border, 2 miles

st of the Path.

5 Chirk Mill to Llandegla

past Dinas Bran and World's End
15½ miles (25.7 km)

The Dyke goes off northwards into the industrial area round Wrexham but the Path goes north-west, high above Llangollen, then crosses the screes of the Eglwyseg and the boggy grouse moors at the watershed between the Dee and the Clywedog. It is a varied section with tough walking and splendid views. A circular walk covers Llangollen.

Two routes are available from the B4500 at Chirk Mill. The *official* one climbs the steep minor road north-westwards to the half-timbered farmhouse at Crogen Wladys. Wild garlic and stitchwort give a white fringe to the verge; there is a fine view up the Ceiriog Valley. Beyond the farm, where the track swings, cross a stile and climb a bank to go north-east. Chirk Castle **52** soon dominates to the east and ahead there is a wide view to Cheshire. You reach a lodge at Tyn-y-groes.

From April to September the alternative *permissive* route to this point runs through the grounds of the Chirk Castle, a National Trust property (see page 94) which you should visit. Go through the iron gate across the B4500 and, after crossing a stream, swing uphill through trees. A stile leads into a meadow with the castle on the ridge above and the Dyke to the west. At the top of the meadow another stile takes you into woods covered in bluebells. Swing west, first on a wider track and then on a drive. At a sign to the coach park go to the north of a stable block and continue to the lodge at Tyn-y-groes. The castle makes a fine prospect for walkers doing this route southwards. The Dyke has continued north-eastwards, *through* a lake created as part of the park's landscaping.

The two routes together form an attractive short *circuit* which can be walked from the castle car park (available only to castle visitors) or from a lay-by near the lime-kilns on the road over the Ceiriog at Chirk Mill: the distance is 2¼ miles (3.6 km).

Continue on the road north-east from Tyn-y-groes, pass a fine half-timbered house with a dovecote, and then cut off a road corner to the west by crossing two fields. After another half mile on a minor road (go on to map on page 85), cross a stile then a field and go down a bank to the Dyke again. You soon reach the A5 by Plas Offa and Offa's Cottages. Take care here when climbing the stile which drops directly on to this busy road.

Chirk Castle, continuously lived in since 1310.

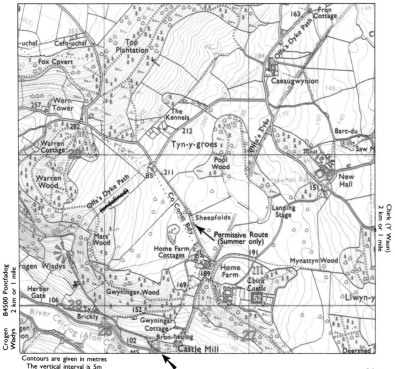

Contours are given in metres
The vertical interval is 5m

83

Contours are given in metres
The vertical interval is 5m

Across the A5 is the last section of Dyke you will walk going north **53** (*see map on page 85, continuing above*). You cross it after two fields and swing east as it goes towards the factories of Acrefair ahead. You soon reach the B5605 (formerly the A483); follow it across the canal, and *immediately* swing west on to the towpath. Below, to the north, is the Dee and a fine railway viaduct on the Wrexham line **54**. A mile of towpath walking is pleasant. The Llangollen Canal **55** is a dead-end remnant of a much larger proposal; it is now used by holiday traffic. Below Froncysyllte, on the A5, you come to a swing footbridge over the canal **56** and another choice of route.

The *official* route of the Path crosses the canal by the swing bridge and then goes out to and down the B5434 to the fine bridge over the Dee. This is *the* best point from which to see the towering 120-foot (40-metre) arches of Telford's Pont Cysyllte canal aqueduct **57**, a wonder of its age (1805), and still one today. A little way up the road from the Dee bridge, a path by houses leads up to the canal again.

As an alternative, you can follow the *permissive* route, continuing on the canal towpath over the aqueduct **57** and so gaining at first hand a sense of its size and of the Dee Valley below, with its bridge and rapids. Those without a good head for heights should use the other route and children should be closely controlled here: there is no barrier on the canal side. At the end of the aqueduct, a small waymarked path swings down and under it to emerge on the B5434. Continue up the road over the Llangollen arm of the canal and take the towpath going west. Cross a footbridge to join the official route.

The two routes described above make a splendid *circuit* of less than 2 miles (3 km). There is parking by the canal at Froncysyllte and next to it by the B road.

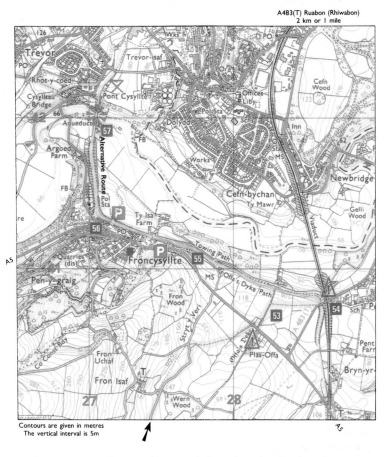

Contours are given in metres
The vertical interval is 5m

Continue on the canal towpath for a few yards after the routes join and then cross a footbridge: the sloping stone slabs eased the way for horses that once towed barges on the canal. Turn away from the canal and cross a field to the remains of another form of transport, a railway embankment. A tunnel a little to the west goes under it and a surfaced path goes out to the A539. The Trevor shop and inn is just to the east, but the Path goes west along the road for some 330 yards before taking a small road north-west for a slightly further distance. Where this road swings sharply, continue ahead into Trevor Hall drive, but soon leave it to climb on a path in dense woodland on the north side.

The climb through the woods is lengthy and steep **A** and includes a gloomy stretch among firs which explains why the spread of coniferous woodland has such a bad reputation among the environmentally minded. After a 550-foot (170-metre) climb you suddenly emerge on to an unfenced road with sheep grazing on a grassy moorland.

85

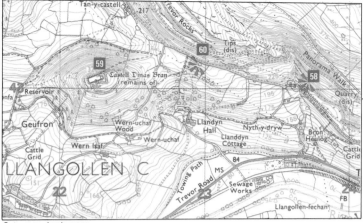

Contours are given in metres
The vertical interval is 5m

The contrast with the scene below is hard to exaggerate. You will be walking on this road, first west and then north, for 3 miles (5 km) and for once it is no hardship. The views to the Dee Valley below, to Castell Dinas Bran ahead, and to the emerging limestone crags to the north are among the wonders of the whole route **58**. Beyond the Dee, the Berwyn Mountains are often snowy. The road has verges and there is no need to walk on the metalled surface, but care must be taken, for in summer the road bears heavy traffic. This, of course, is why it was developed as a Panorama Walk for visitors to the resort area of Llangollen. During our early Offa's Dyke explorations we coined the term Precipice Walk for this section, for obvious reasons.

The view from here **60** alters as you go west: Dinas Bran **59** on its hill increasingly dominates and Llangollen is seen clearly below. Halfway along the road stretch, a small turning goes off to the south and from this Castell Dinas Bran can be climbed (see circuit route on page 93). Your road now swings north and the views are to the hills west across the Eglwyseg tributary of the Dee. Descend a little, pass two farms and then go through a gate (labelled Bryn Goleu) on the east of the road. This crosses a gully with a rushing stream coming down from the crags above and then takes to the open hillside way above the tree line on a narrow path on the scree **61 B**. This section calls for a good sense of balance but it is quite safe in all but the worst weather, when continuing on the narrow road to World's End is the better option. Certainly the Path is much safer than it was in earlier

Contours are given in metres
The vertical interval is 5m

days, as lengthy use has widened the ledge in the scree. It is an exhilarating walk, with wide views to the west, the crags above, rock violets in the scree at your feet, and probably kestrels and jackdaws, which nest in the crevices, overhead.

The Path continues over three areas of scree separated by stream-fed gullies. After the third area of scree you reach a junction of paths. Inviting though the upper path may seem, your Path is the lower one; it drops a little, first following a single line of old trees and then crosses a high ladder stile before it passes through the remains of a very old plantation **C**. Below, on the road, you will see the fine, early 17th century manor house of Plas Uchaf **62**. Cross a stile and pass through a dense patch of firs, from which you come out by the falls and horse-shoe bend in the road known as World's End **63**. The spot attracts many picnickers and artists but has no amenities.

The Path now climbs the Minera road north for a long mile on to the desolate moors of Cyrn-y-Brain. At most times it is a quiet road but on summer weekends it can have queues of vehicles, many not expecting the narrow road or the severe climbs, so the walker may have a hard time. Take a look down the valley from just above the horseshoe at World's End: the view is rewarding.

There is no obvious landmark to tell you where to leave the road to cross the moors to the west, so you must watch for the wooden signpost. On the moors there is a clear track, with some board walks, climbing to the woods on the horizon across the soft peaty bog **D**. This and the Hatterrall, on the Black Mountains, are the only parts of the Path where the Pennine Way walker will readily recognise the conditions. It is not comfortable but at least there is a clear route. In mist, however, a compass bearing and a close watch on the map are most advisable. In fine weather larks sing and grouse are to be seen here. This is Wynnstay Estate country, and not long before the opening of the Path we were in a party that was turned back by an armed gamekeeper. These days the chief menace is from unauthorised motorcycle scramblers.

Near the top of the moorland climb, you cross a stile and soon drop through extensive plantations of young conifers. While these were being planted the route was almost impossible to detect, and eventually the trees will grow into the gloomy forests of all such plantations, but for some years the route will be clear and not too overgrown. The surface is still spongy, however, and planking is being laid at the worst spots to stop you being engulfed in peaty mud **E** (see map on page 91).

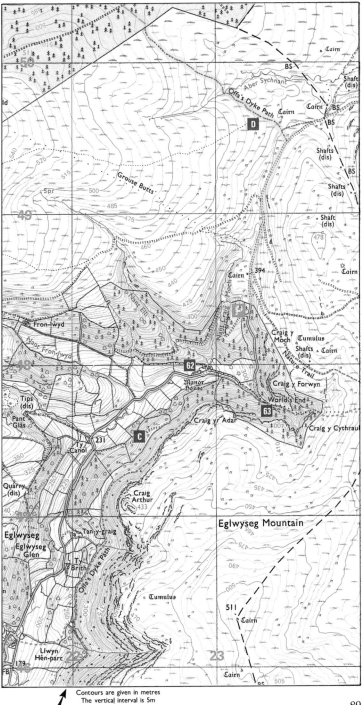

Contours are given in metres
The vertical interval is 5m

You drop to a conduit from the Pendinas Reservoir, follow this a little way west, descend a short muddy dingle, cross a forestry track, and then go down a lovely grassy track in the woods (*see map on page 91 continuing below*). The track crosses a second forestry road, with a deep gorge below to the west, and you soon see Nant yr Hafod (formerly Hafod Bilston) beneath you **64**. The old house and barns have been beautifully converted, and have attractive gardens on the banks of the stream. The Path reaches the drive down a steep bank and through a gate with 'Llwybr Clawdd Offa, Offa's Dyke Path' picked out in the ironwork.

Briefly follow the road north past the buildings and then climb the side of a field going north-west. Over the brow the Path drops under a line of buzzing cables, crosses a branch of the River Alyn and rises to the busy A525 by the east side of a garden. Go west for a few yards and then up a short path between houses to a small road; west again and you are soon on the A5104 at Pen-y-stryt. The Crown Inn is just to the south-west and the main street of Llandegla village lies ahead. (The Inn marked here is not now a hostelry.)

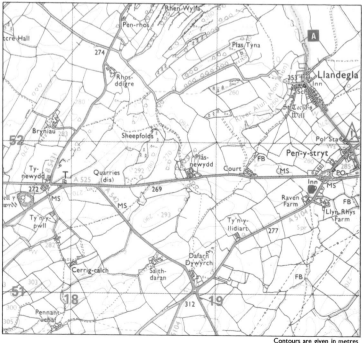

Contours are given in metres
The vertical interval is 5m

The Old Rectory in the village of Llandegla, with its interesting chimneys.

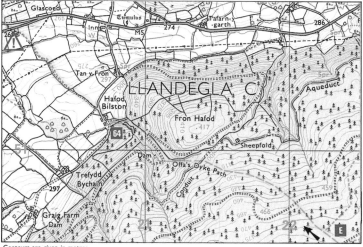

Contours are given in metres
The vertial interval is 5m

91

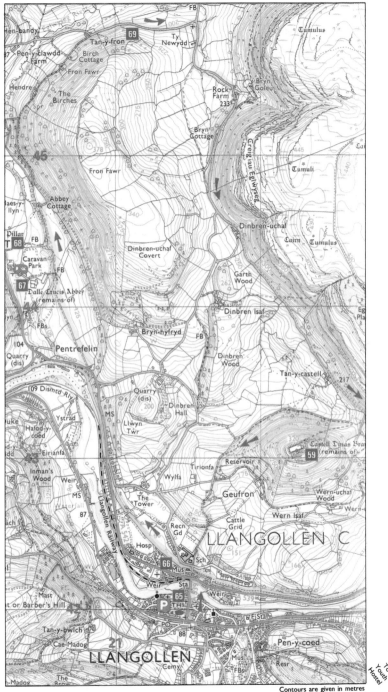

Contours are given in metres
The vertical interval is 5m

A CIRCULAR WALK IN THE VALE OF LLANGOLLEN

6 miles (9.5 km)

From Llangollen's main car park (grid ref. 214 420) follow the principal thoroughfare, Castell Street, north over the Dee Bridge **65** turning right and left with the Wharf Hill road to join the canal towpath on the left. Pass the Canal Exhibition Centre **66** and the site of the Llangollen International Eisteddfod, and continue under two bridges (notice the grooves worn into the abutments by tow ropes). At the next bridge (access to the Motor Museum) go right and then along the A542. After 80 yards take the footpath signposted left. From the stile follow the track beside a hedge, via two stiles, with delightful hill views ahead. Arriving at a three-way footpath sign above the wooded bank, take the opportunity of paying a visit to the ruins of Valle Crucis Abbey **67** and the Pillar of Eliseg **68** (see page 98).

The route continues north and, after a stile, follows the headland of an arable field to a stile beside Abbey Cottage. Turn right, from the gate go left along the track beside the conifer plantation, and beyond Hendre relax briefly upon the seat in memory of a 'Bill Fairclough, who loved this hillside': clearly a man of discrimination! The emphasis of the view here **69** soon switches from the greens of the Horseshoe Pass Valley to the gleaming white cliffs and scree of Creigiau Eglwyseg, as the route joins a minor road continuing east to a T-junction. Turn south, rising past Rock Farm to accompany Offa's Dyke Path past Dinbren-uchaf and Tan-y-castell Farms, then take the road right at a cattle grid beneath Trevor Rocks. Cross the sturdy stile right, initially descending, then head west up the steepening pasture to a stile giving access to Castell Dinas Bran **59** (see pages 96 and 98). Linger for a while at this delectable viewpoint by the castle ruins before making the steep zigzagging descent down the grassy west ridge to enter a lane (through a gate) at Tirionfa. This leads across Wern Lane to Geufron, where a wicket gate gives access to a field path down beside a hedge. Cross a metalled lane and continue via a further wicket gate into a fenced passage down past Llangollen Secondary School to reach the Wharf Hill road.

Chirk Castle 52

The castle, an important feature of the views from the Path for some miles, is owned by the National Trust and is open to visitors during the spring and summer (times and dates should be checked). It was a late Marcher stronghold, completed in 1310, after the defeat of the last native Prince of Wales. The outer appearance, of high sandstone walls with massive drum towers enclosing a courtyard, has changed little. However, these first impressions are rather misleading for, like Powis Castle, Chirk has been restored and converted into a stately home over the ensuing centuries. Inside you will see elegant plasterwork, furniture, tapestries and pictures, and there are beautiful formal gardens. The superb wrought-iron entrance gates of 1712–19 are by the Davies brothers; but these are at the main entrance from Chirk town, not on the 'permissive' Offa's Dyke Path route.

The Pont Cysyllte Aqueduct 57 and the Llangollen Canal 55

The canal system in the area is complex, for what was intended as a major link-up of the Mersey, Dee and Severn was never completed. Thus the aqueduct, built by Thomas Telford in 1795 to 1805, one of the great innovative masterpieces of the Industrial Revolution, ended by carrying only a relatively minor branch of the Shropshire Union system. Other aqueducts in this system, such as that at Chirk, are built on stone arches, but the canal at Pont Cysyllte is carried in a 1,000-foot (300-metre) cast-iron trough on 18 stone piers above the River Dee, which from here looks like a mountain stream as it rushes over rapids more than 120 feet (35 metres) below. To the south, a high embankment, longer than the aqueduct, leads from the site of canal wharves at Froncysyllte. At the north end, where the main canal to Wrexham and Chester should have been built, a branch goes west to Llangollen and Llantysilio, where Telford designed the crescent-shaped Horseshoe Falls to supply water to the system. The towpath of the branch makes an attractive walking route to Llangollen, over 4 miles (6 km) away, where it can be linked to the circular walk described on page 93.

Llangollen

The town is one of the main tourist centres near the Offa's Dyke Path, offering a variety of accommodation including, a little to the east, a youth hostel at Tyndwr Hall – a large Victorian villa

The Pont Cysyllte, Telford's aqueduct, dating from the end of the 18th century, over the Dee Valley.

with attractive half-timbering and elaborate internal panelling and plasterwork. Llangollen is famous for its International Eisteddfod, held each July, which offers many major concerts as well as competitive events for singers, folk artists and dancers from all over the world.

The main visual attraction is the town's setting, with Castell Dinas Bran **59** rising to the north and the crags of the Eglwyseg (traversed by our Path) beyond, and the eastern end of the Berwyn Mountains to the south. The four-arched bridge over the Dee **65** may date in part from the 14th century or earlier, but it has frequently been widened to take additional traffic. The former railway, now in part a preserved steam line, passed under it. The views up and down the Dee are attractive. The church of St Collen was much altered externally by its Victorian restoration, but inside there are fine medieval hammerbeam roofs.

Llangollen's best-known residents were no doubt the 'Ladies of Llangollen', Lady Eleanor Butler and Miss Sarah Ponsonby, two well-to-do Irish ladies who, dissatisfied with their home life, settled at Plas Newydd **70**, near the town centre, in 1780.

They embellished the plain stone house with romantic Gothic and other period pastiche details, and laid out gardens including the semi-wild glen near the house. Many of the features and furnishings of the house, and some garden structures, remain, and the whole, now owned by the local council, is open to the public. Their writings, including accounts of tremendous walking feats, are still widely read.

Castell Dinas Bran 59

The isolated hilltop was occupied by an Iron Age hill fort, but its ramparts were partly destroyed when the castle was built in the 13th century. This was a Welsh castle of the princes of north Powys, but it was probably occupied only until the wars later in the same century, when it was burnt and abandoned. Much of the ruined walls and towers still survives. The spectacular viewpoint was unsuitable for civilian settlement, so the town of Llangollen was established in the valley below.

Valle Crucis Abbey 67

The abbey was established in 1201 in the valley of the Eglwyseg River, a northern tributary of the Dee, by Madog ap Gruffyd Maelor, probably the builder of Castell Dinas Bran. Its peaceful valley site, below the foothills of the Eglwyseg, is as lovely a setting as those of Tintern and Llanthony, near the southern part of the Path, but alas, in recent years, a large caravan site has been allowed to develop far too near the ruins. If you look away from that, then the Cistercian church, with its west and east ends still intact, and the range of buildings south of it (well preserved by later agricultural use) form a picture of great beauty. The Chapter House, built about 1400, has fine mouldings and tracery. The site is in the care of Cadw and is open all the year.

The Pillar of Eliseg 68

This feature, a quarter of a mile to the north of the abbey, is the shaft of a cross built on an earlier tumulus mound. A long Latin inscription, now much decayed, celebrates the descent and achievements of Eliseg, 'who united the inheritance of Powys' and may have had successes against King Offa himself, and of Eliseg's great-grandson, Cyngen, who erected the stone in the 9th century.

The ruins of the 13th century Cistercian abbey of Valle Crucis in the valley of the Eglwyseg River.

The view from Castell Dinas Bran north to the Eglwyseg crags.

6 Llandegla to Bodfari

via Clwyd Gate and Jubilee Tower
17½ miles (28 km)

This is an exhilarating moorland walk along a range of rounded hills of hard Silurian Shales, with fine Iron Age forts and even more striking views – from Snowdon to Cheshire. Unlike the Black Mountains there is a series of climbs, though you hardly go over 1,800 feet (550 metres), so it is quite a test to do it in one day. The walk can be broken by descending to villages, such as Llanarmon-yn-Ial, or by using transport from the Ruthin to Mold main road (which crosses a little less than halfway along the section). The fine landscape of the 22-mile (35-km) ridge of the open and colourful Clwydian Range, with its striking escarpment on the eastern side, was designated as an area of outstanding natural beauty in 1985.

First, however, you cross 3 miles (5 km) of fertile farmland to the south-east of the hill range. Go down Llandegla street, past the shop, and turn off down the narrow lane between the church and the former Hand Inn. The next section of route is quite tricky to follow **A**. Cross a stile into a long field with the River Alyn to your west. Go over a footbridge and then the path ahead cuts off a bend in the river. The river is beside you again after a bridge across a tributary. You cross an earth bridge where the two streams diverge and continue north as before along a pasture field bounded on the east by the smaller stream, now only a ditch. At the top, a turning west along a muddy farm lane, which does, however, sport cowslips in season, soon leads out to the B5431. You will have noted low outcrops of limestone in this section: some contain caves and there have been finds confirming prehistoric occupation **71**. If you can attend to more than the navigational problems you will note the east side of the Clwydians ahead of you and the cone of Llantysilio Mountain, north of Llangollen, behind.

Across the road you follow the drive to Chweleiriog Farm. The Path used to go right through the farmyard but a well waymarked rerouting now turns off at a limestone outcrop and takes it to the south of the farm, up three fields and by a wood. At the top, cross a stile in the hedge, turn a little south of west and go out to a little road just above the small farm of Tyddyn-tlodion.

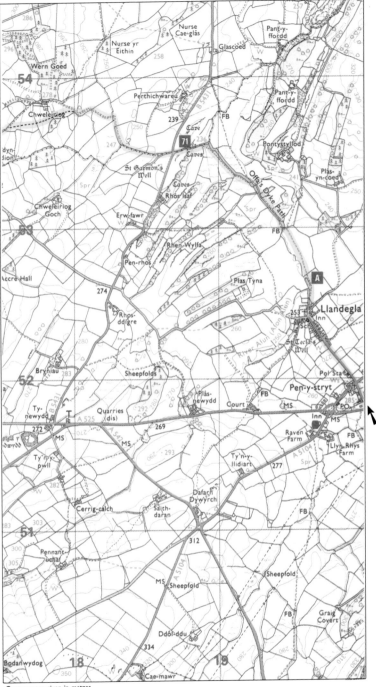

Contours are given in metres
The vertical interval is 10m

101

You go north on this road, with its steep violet-clad banks, for half a mile to the point where it reaches open moors and swings west. Here the Path continues north, by a fence and wood, and climbs past a transmitter station. You are soon on the first of your climbs of a Clwydian hill, straight up the steep slopes of Moel y Plâs. From its ridge there is a fine view south down to the waters of Llyn Gweryd in its surrounding woodland **72**. Cross a fence and contour through the heather and bilberries, the natural vegetation of most of these slopes, to avoid dropping into the steep cwm to the west. You soon descend steeply to old pigsties at the top of the narrow road which comes up, from the east, from the village of Llanarmon-yn-Ial, 1½ miles (2.5 km) away **73**. This pleasant place, with the Raven Inn and other facilities, is a good spot to break the Clwydian walk.

The Path, however, continues north-west from the col above and west of the village to skirt below the top of the next hill in the range, Moel Llanfair **74**. From this hillside **75** the old county town of Ruthin (see page 111), with its red stone castle, dominates the vale below to the west as it will do for some miles. Round a corner one of the wide and ugly new EEC-financed agricultural roads is reached and must be followed east uphill to the slopes below the top of Moel Gyw. This used to be a pretty path: how much so can be seen by comparing it with the one on which you turn north off the road. Time will weather their raw gashes to some extent, but such roads have undoubtedly brought a touch of the factory to these remote landscapes.

The footpath soon joins another wide track to complete the contouring of the west side of Moel Gyw. Where this track turns east, you cross a stile and swing west over a field above a wood to the south **B**. The Path is not well marked on the ground and you must cross a col between twin small summits. In the next field go down the north side to reach a drive above a farm (see map on page 104). This last section needs careful navigation. The drive leads east to the main A494 Ruthin to Mold road, which has a bus service, by the Clwyd Gate Inn and Restaurant (not open in 1994; may reopen in 1995). There are plans for a by-pass road here.

Turn east along the road for a short distance. Your route continues on a drive to a house on the north side, a relief from the vergeless busy main road. The original route of the Path went directly north up the hillside of Gyrn leading to Moel Eithinen, and this is still a right of way. Following a lengthy dispute, however, the Offa's Dyke Path was diverted to con-

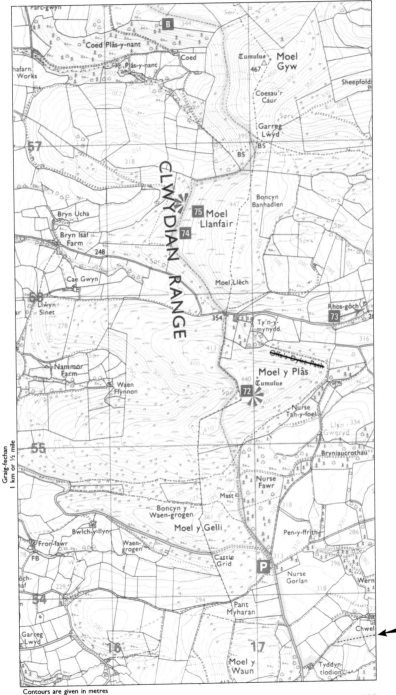

Graig-fechan
1 km or ⅓ mile

Contours are given in metres
The vertical interval is 10m

103

tinue along the drive, below the house and a most attractive garden, and then by the west fork at two succeeding junctions. You are now on a pretty path which goes through a small larch wood and then contours above Moel-eithinen Farm. The views to the east are of the Alyn Valley and the limestone hills beyond.

Beyond the top of a rise you turn sharply west by a wall, soon with a wood to your north. The Path rises gradually to the col between Moel Eithinen, to the south, and Foel Fenlli **76** to the north. By a fence turn sharp north towards the steep slopes and ramparts of the latter. Climb by a fir wood, go down to a gully and then start the main, sharp climb.

The route used to go over the top of Fenlli but, to reduce erosion of the hill fort, walkers are now asked to skirt to the westernmost point of the ramparts **C** and then descend gradually to the east of the pass and the road and car park at Bwlch Penbarra. You may well welcome the strong invitation to avoid part of one of the steepest climbs on the range!

The next 1¾ miles (2.8 km) of the route climb to the highest point on the Clwydian range. The car park at its southern end, and the area's country park status, make this a favourite stroll for weekend family parties – leading to considerable erosion

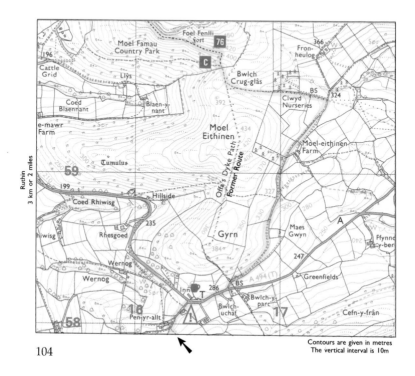

Contours are given in metres
The vertical interval is 10m

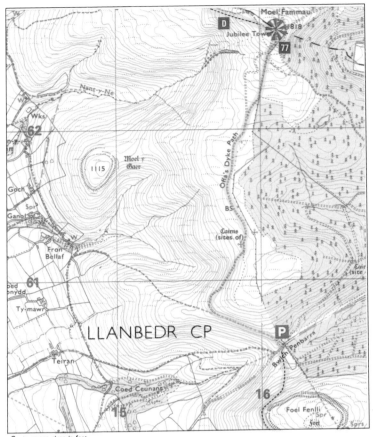

Contours are given in feet
The vertical interval is 25ft

problems. Clwyd County Council has responded successfully by gravelling the main path and using tree branches to edge it.

The Path first goes north-west and then swings north to the summit of Moel Fammau (or Famau, the 'Mother Mountain') **77**: there are other walked paths a little to the east but this is the right of way. The final climb is quite steep to the millstone grit top at 1,818 feet (554 metres), with the ruins of the Jubilee Tower, a pyramid erected in 1810 to mark the Jubilee of George III, but never completed. It partly collapsed because of insubstantial foundations and was rather a mess until tidied up in 1970 as a European Conservation Year project, when a set of toposcopes was installed showing places visible from the top: including Snowdon, 35 miles (56 km) away and Liverpool, 20 miles (32 km) away. The Ordnance Survey uses the site for tracking satellites for navigation and mapping work, linked with stations in Europe.

From the summit the Path goes steeply downhill, a little north of west. From here **78** you can see the defensive rings of the hill fort of Moel y Gaer below to the south. Steps are provided to ease the way and limit erosion **D**. As you continue down after the first steep drop, a well-built stone wall is just by you to the east. Then turn sharply north, and climb again; the moorland tarn of Pwll-y-Rhos is just over the wall to the east **79**. Moel Dywyll is the next summit with a big cairn on the ridge **80**. The Path then drops down, with the fence and wall still to the east. The town of Denbigh (see page 111), with its prominent castle, dominates the valley to the west, and to the east are the reservoirs above Cilcain and the Alyn Valley.

The succession of short climbs and descents through heather slopes continues northwards now, up Moel Llys-y-coed. You swing north-east near the top and suddenly the next two hills and hill forts, Moel Arthur **82** and Penycloddiau to the north-west, come into view across a deep valley. This is the best place from which to appreciate the extraordinary formation of the former, at 1,494 feet (455 metres). It is a perfect, steep-sided but quite small cone, with impressive triple lines of defences.

Before climbing Moel Arthur's slopes, however, you have a very steep drop **E** into the valley south of it, which carries a little road and where a few cars can be parked. The Path used to go directly north, very steeply up to the top of Moel Arthur, but the usual erosion problem has led the county council to divert the Path over the eastern shoulder of the hill, a kissing gate and a clear track marking the route **F**. It is quite simple to go to the top from the point where the Path reaches the ridge. The route is less steep on the north side, especially after the first stile, as it drops north-west down a grassy slope to another of the minor roads crossing the range of hills.

A few yards up the road is a car park with a large forestry plantation below it clinging to the west slopes of the summit range. The Path leaves the car park by a gate and you must be careful not to stray on to any of the forestry tracks **G**. Follow the high footpath going north of west just below the east fence of the trees and above all the forestry rides (see map on page 109). In half a mile you rise to just below the southern end of the fort of Penycloddiau **83** and then enter it by swinging north up through one of the original entrances. Penycloddiau differs from all the other hill forts in the range by its size. The interior

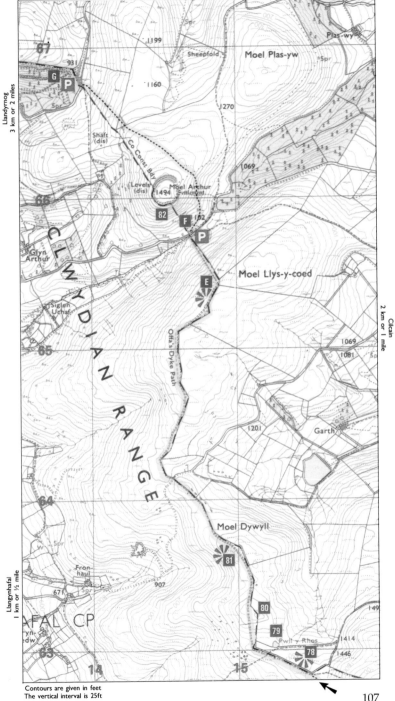

Contours are given in feet
The vertical interval is 25ft

107

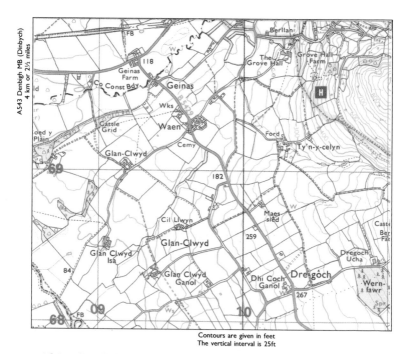

Contours are given in feet
The vertical interval is 25ft

within the defences is nearly half a mile long from north to south. The Path (*see map on page 109, continuing above*) now goes up the middle of the hill fort, but a full circuit of the earthwork is attractive if time permits. From the southern end **84** there is a good view south to Moel Arthur and the Jubilee Tower.

The Path now descends to Bodfari, falling more than 1,300 feet in less than 3 miles (5 km). The rest of the stretch on the crest follows a wide track on a ridge, passing a memorial stile to Arthur Roberts, Ramblers' Association and Offa's Dyke Path pioneer, and dropping steeply to a junction of tracks at a col. Here **85**, three-quarters of a mile from Penycloddiau, is an old grove of pines. Moel y Parc, with a high television mast, is ahead of you to the north, but you leave the ridge by walking west on a farm track falling away from the col.

Ty Newydd is the first farm you pass, where you cross a stream, go up a short rise, and immediately take the left (south) fork to follow an open moorland path with a steep hillside above and a stream to the south below. Where, in half a mile, this swings sharply north, you continue ahead on a short grass path. Some care in navigation is needed over the final mile into Bodfari: the open Clwyds may have rusted your sense of negotiating fields **H**! Cross a stile ahead of you and descend the

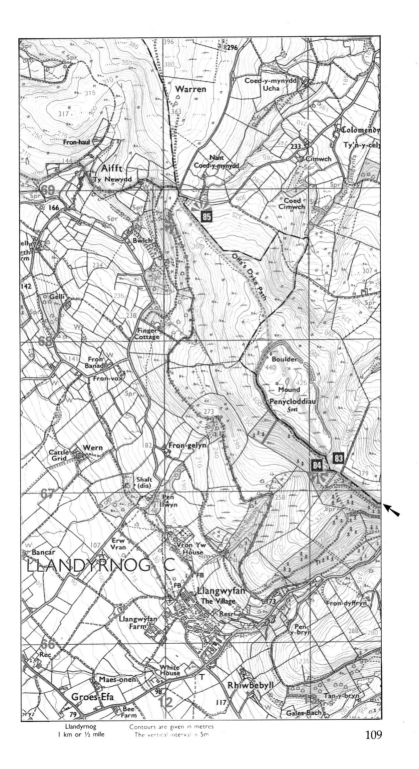

Llandyrnog
1 km or ½ mile

Contours are given in metres
The vertical interval is 5m

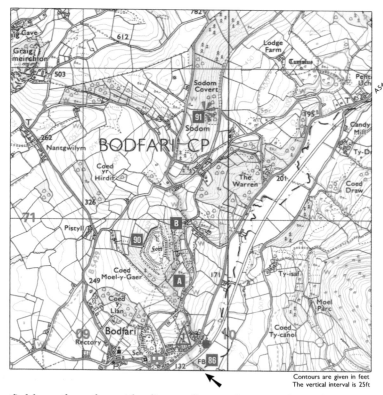

Contours are given in feet
The vertical interval is 25ft

field on the other side diagonally north-west, through gorse, aiming for the large house, The Grove, which you can see ahead. Go over a further stile, then cross the top of a small sloping field and swing right (north) over a series of stiles east of The Grove to reach a small road by its drive.

Go west down the road, north at a T-junction, and immediately west again, with Bodfari church high on the slope ahead. Where this road turns south, a path ahead leads across the River Wheeler, then across the track of the former Mold to Denbigh and Ruthin railway **86**, and goes out to the main A541 at Bodfari.

Nearby towns

Nearby towns offer useful facilities as well as interesting things to see. On the east side, Wrexham, about 9 miles (14.5 km) from Llandegla, though an industrial centre, has the magnificent church of St Giles, substantial remains of Wat's Dyke on the outskirts, and the National Trust mansion of Erddig to the south.

Mold, further north, 7 miles (11 km) on the A494 from where the Path crosses, also has a fine church, St Mary's, and a motte and bailey castle. It is perhaps most notable for Theatr Clwyd, one of the best appointed new theatres, which is sited with Clwyd County Council's offices: it certainly has the best view from its foyer, and it is a memorable experience to watch the range of the Clwyds spread before you in the gathering dusk as you wait for the play to start.

To the west, Ruthin, some 4 miles (6.5 km) on the A494, retains much of its old town centre and of its castle, both the medieval ruins and a 19th century house, much used for 'medieval banquets', but not usually open to the public. St Peter's Church is basically 14th century and, like Chirk Castle, has lovely wrought iron gates by the Davies brothers.

Denbigh, 3 miles (5 km) from Bodfari, is the most spectacular of these towns on its steeply sloping site. The castle was built by the Marcher de Lacy family after the defeat of the Welsh princes in 1282 and an almost complete circuit of town walls survives. There are several historic churches, as well as the unique remains of an unfinished Elizabethan church.

A welcome awaits you at Bodfari Post Office, as well as at other villages along the Path.

A circular walk via Moel Fammau

7 miles (11 km)

Generous roadside car parking may be found in the Alyn Valley below Cilcain (grid ref. 187 652). Walk uphill (west) along the Cilcain road, and continue along the initially confined footpath signposted left at the sharp right-hand bend. Keep to the edge of the ensuing fields, cross the stiles, and watch for the stile into the wooded bank that leads to a narrow descending path. Pass above the landscaped dam on Afon Gain to join the minor road. Go left, dipping and rising across the valley, then follow the road right at the junction, signposted 'Cilcain'. Follow the bridle lane continuation of this road, an old drover's way.

After the first two reservoirs there is a gate, then beyond the approach to Garth take a bridle gate left, the old way sweeping round the upper reservoir, the resort of local fly fishermen **87**. The path fords a side stream then rises west, along a broken-walled lane, to join a surfaced track going left to the pass. From the gate go left (south-east) along the ridgetop route of Offa's Dyke Path, passing on the way the handsome cairn on Moel Dywyll.

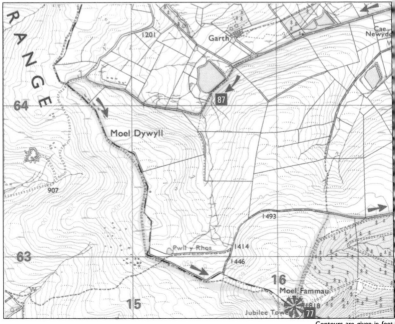

Contours are given in feet
The vertical interval is 25ft

The walk, having begun upon the Carboniferous Limestone, graduates on to Silurian Shales, and reaches its high point with the final steep climb up to the Jubilee Tower on Moel Fammau **77**. Fammau, the 'Mother Mountain', holds a gracious maternal dominance over the Vale of Clwyd and is one of the prime viewpoints of North Wales.

Follow the Cilcain path north, down beside the forestry, and branch east upon reaching the cross lane at the foot of the plantation. This bridleway descends into a lane that passes Castell, via three gates, and Ffrith Farm, then goes left along the metalled road to Bryn Alyn. Cross at the junction into the initially confined path waymarked on the Loggerheads road-sign. The footpath descends directly to the Alyn footbridge by way of stiles, past a secluded cottage. From the 'wall squeezer', rise left to contour north by an old leat (a man-made watercourse). This dramatic path cuts a shelf course across the limestone cliff above the summer-dry Alyn River, passing over a footbridge spanning a deep rift cavern. Keep with the dry leat on its startling course, with increasingly impressive cliff scenery **88**, past a shallow cave, to reach the minor road (teas 200 yards on the right), then turn left down into the valley to finish.

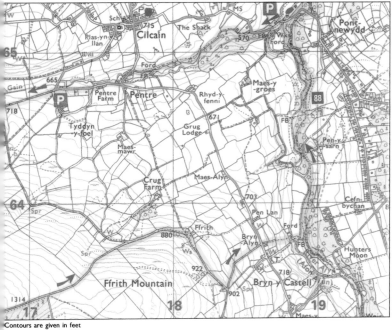

Contours are given in feet
The vertical interval is 25ft

Contours are given in metres
The vertical interval is 5m

A CIRCULAR WALK VIA PENYCLODDIAU

5¼ miles (9 km)

From the Llangwyfan forestry car park (grid ref. 139 668) enter the forestry plantation, accompanying Offa's Dyke Path to the right, go up to the impressive 'Dyke-like' ramparts of Penyclod-diau hill fort **83** and on down to the pass at 1,004 feet (306 metres). Turn obliquely south-west, away from the Path, along the contouring track with its memorable prospects over the Vale of Clwyd **89**, via a sequence of six gates, and on to the hill road above Llangwyfan Mental Hospital. Follow the road left, with the option of cutting short the walk up the forestry track at the first (right-hand) bend (4 miles/6.5 km).

One hundred yards after the second (left-hand) bend enter the field on your right, at a gate. Mount the pasture bank to pass through the gate to the left of the beech trees, also keeping left of Fron-dyffryn, and pass through its access gateway. Climb half right along a trackway to a stile (beside angled double gates) then follow the track on its basically contouring course, via two further gates, on to the next hill road above Glyn Arthur, and go left to the Star Crossing car park.

Re-joining Offa's Dyke Path at the kissing gate, head northwards once more, over the shoulder of Moel Arthur **82**, to conclude this joyous excursion on the Clwydian Hills.

The Clwydian hill forts

Hill forts of the Iron Age, the period in Britain just before the Roman conquest starting in AD 43, have been encountered already on or near the Path, for instance at Pentwyn at the south end of the Hatterrall, at Burfa north of Kington and at Old Oswestry. However, the Clwydians have a whole series of outstanding examples. Directly on the line of the Path are Foel Fenlli **76**, Moel Arthur **82** and Penycloddiau **83**, with *two* called Moel y Gaer (one south-west of Moel Fammau **78**, the other north of Bodfari **90**) and the northernmost, Moel Hiraddug, just west of the walking route.

Most are protected by two or more encircling ramparts and ditches, usually with visible remains of interned entrances, where the banks turn inwards to provide guardposts. In several of the larger enclosures there are also traces of round houses.

The patchwork landscape of the Vale of Clwyd, looking towards the west from

nycloddiau.

7 Bodfari to Prestatyn

passing through Rhuallt
12 miles (19 km)

'What a pity the north end is so boring. Might as well miss it out.' This is sometimes said by those planning to walk the Path – but wrongly, as you will find out. There are several minor road stretches and the end of the trail is at Prestatyn, a 20th century holiday resort, but the section has its share of hills, in the north of the Clwydian Range, and a variety of walking within one day that is unusual even for this Path. The distant views of the sea and Snowdonia should be enough even for satiated walkers!

A good supply of energy and navigational skills is needed as you set off from Bodfari. Opposite the Downing Arms, at the north end of the village, the Path climbs up the very steep minor road going west from the A541. You reach a junction by a house and continue the climb by a diagonal path almost opposite up a field **A**. Cross a stile at its northmost corner and contour north in woods below the top of Moel y Gaer hill fort **90**. Across the Wheeler Valley rises Moel y Parc, the hill with the television mast. Soon you rise to skirt above a house, then quickly drop to cross its drive and the field below to reach a small road. Go left (north) on this, and also at the following fork **B**. You reach a hairpin in the little road and go forward over a stile here. Then go up the west side of two fields and the middle of the next to a small road just west of Adwywynt Farm.

The next stretch is much more straightforward. Go east on the road by the farm and immediately take the turn climbing to the north, past hillsides clad in gorse. From the viewpoint **91**, west is the Vale of Clwyd and, if the weather is clear, Snowdonia and the sea, and to the east a glimpse of Caerwys, a 14th century planned town, with a rectangular street plan, that never quite took off. To the south there looms the bulk of Moel y Gaer **90** which you have just skirted. After more than half a mile (and note, on the west, a well tapping a spring) the road swings east with the Path continuing straight ahead up the steep slope of Cefn Du **92**. You have only two fields to climb up to the top of this minor Clwydian outlier, and a similar distance down. On the descent keep some distance from the fence to the west to find the stile between the two fields as the route here is not well trodden. Rejoin the road at the bottom of the hill and continue

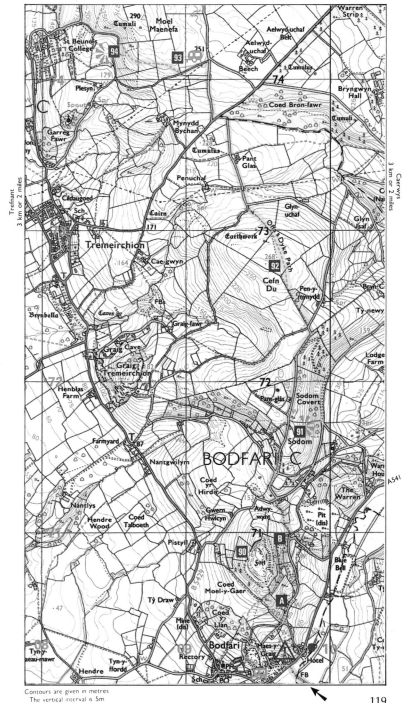

Contours are given in metres
The vertical interval is 5m

119

north on it to a T-junction, where you go west and then immediately north up a similar minor road. At the top, and after two-thirds of a mile on roads, a track leads you west past a small caravan site. Soon you cross a stile on the north side and climb round the slopes of Moel Maenefa **93**, keeping well below the summit to the north.

Descend the south-west slopes of Moel Maenefa on a narrow path through gorse so thick that the coconut smell can be overpowering. From here **94**, looking westwards you should see the tiny cathedral city of St Asaph (see page 126) with the mountains beyond and the sea at Llandudno. A stile by the corner of a fence and a path ahead soon lead to an enclosed track going west to a minor road. Descend this but, after one field, cross a stile to go north again towards Maen Efa Farm (now unoccupied). The Path skirts under and one field to the west of it **C**, before following a new route resulting from the new A55 Rhuallt by-pass (this route has still – 1994 – a 'temporary' status). Bear north-west down two fields to a footbridge below the embankment of the new road. Continue, now north-easterly, up to the top corner of a long field and swing west over a massive new footbridge **95** over the trunk road. Continue on the minor (but Roman) road which quickly drops to the junction of the former A55 and the B5429 at the Smithy Arms, Rhuallt.

Banks of gorse are found on many of the northern Clwydian hills.

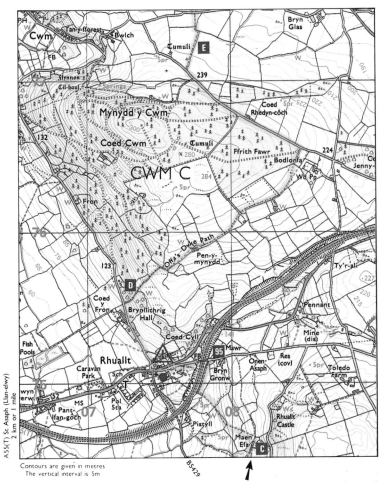

Go north here on the narrow road for one-third of a mile and then, over a stile, very steeply north-east up a path through a patch of woodland and beyond by gorse clumps and foxglove covered wall. This slope of Mynydd y Cwm **D** proves that the Clwyds have not yet finished with you! Beyond a stile at the corner of a firwood, you take a broad green track which skirts above Pen-y-mynydd Farm, and then follows the drive to the road above Bodlonfa.

Turn left to follow the road north-west on the hill crest for about half a mile. Just beyond where the wood to the south-west ends, go down two fields on the opposite side of the road **E**. Then cross a small lane and go diagonally across the next field, aiming for the easternmost buildings of the settlement ahead, Marian Cwm. Before it, descend to a dip, then up steps and between gardens to the road. Continue on the path across the road by the letter box, cross a stile and go diagonally up the rocky slopes of Marian Ffrith **96**. From the top you will have a wide panorama of the sea to the west and north.

The Path descends the north slopes of Marian Ffrith aiming just to the east of a farm **F**. Join its track and turn west past the buildings. Cross a stile a little further on, on the north side of the lane, descend a dip in the field, and continue along the west side of the next field. Turn north-east on a green farm track to cross a small road and descend two more fields: aim at a 'finger' of trees **G**, the remains of an old hedge, and follow the west side of this out to an enclosed bridleway. This leads east, past verges rich in cowslips, to the remains of the Marian Mill complex **97**. Join a surfaced track to go north past a reservoir, a canalised waterway and falls, and a water wheel. Continue under the abutments of a former bridge to a horseshoe bend in the road and take the upper (north) exit. Where the road swings east, take the path that rises ahead, just east of a pretty dingle, to the busy A5151.

Looking north to the sea from the northern slopes of Marian Ffrith.

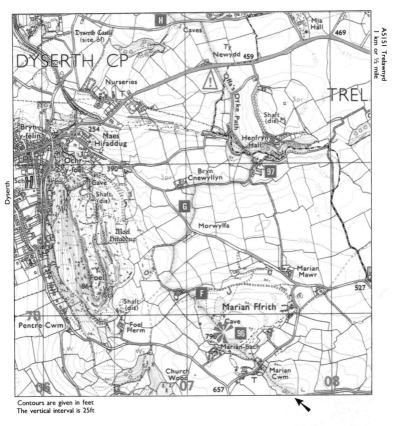

Contours are given in feet
The vertical interval is 25ft

The Path goes up a field just east of Ty Newydd Farm; then down the next field to a minor road and follows it west for about 150 yards. You will see Gop Hill **98** (see page 127) to the east, and to the south-west Moel Hiraddug, the most northerly Clwydian hill, now disfigured by quarrying. Steps lead north, up a bank from the minor road, and then you cross a field near a line of pylons: an acorn sign on a pole shows the way **H**. Aim for a red brick house (see map on page 125) and go across a series of fields to a road just where the drive from the house comes out. Go west and immediately north and then north-east **I**, by a kissing gate, to the drive to Red Roofs, a cliffside bungalow. Before you reach its gates, another kissing gate leads to a path skirting east of the house. Take the lower fork just beyond and suddenly you realise that you are on Prestatyn Cliffs **99** with the town and sea more than 500 feet (150 m) below. The end is in sight.

Before that, though, you will enjoy the traverse of 1½ miles (2.5 km) of clifftop. The Path leads through gorse slopes to an old quarry and skirts its top. It is important *not* to be carried down into the quarry **J**. Beyond its end take the top fork at a junction and climb steeply to the ridge above the ancient oak woods of Coed yr Esgob through the gorse – and orchids. You are a little below the top of the 700-foot (210-metre) cliff on a narrow path with a very steep fall below **100**. Coming south, on rising to this point, the magnificent view west to Llandudno, Snowdonia and even Anglesey opens up **101**. For the north-bound walker, the last section of Path slopes steeply down to come out on a small road.

To the north there is a small park but you swing south on Bishopswood Road **K** and quickly round a horseshoe, with a picnic site and room for a few cars, to the junction with Mount Ida Road and Fford-las at the top end of Prestatyn **102**. Follow Fford-las and its continuations – High Street and Bastion Road – downhill for more than a mile to the sea. At the junction with Meliden Road there is a display board about the Dyke and Path. High Street has the shops and Tourist Information Centre. Cross the footbridge over the railway, go down Bastion Road and reach the sea at last by Rhuddlan D.C.'s Offa's Dyke Centre, and the stone **103** put up to mark the end of the Path. There is an apocryphal story that Fford-las and its continuation mark the line of the Dyke, and there is a walkers' tradition that, on reaching the beach, you take off your footwear and wade out, on the exact line of the Path **104**, as far as you dare.

PRESTATYN HILLSIDE WALKS

Clwyd County Council has established a compact network of waymarked paths linking up with Offa's Dyke Path, around the steep limestone escarpment above Prestatyn, and based upon the viewpoint car park half a mile north of Gwaenysgor (grid ref. 074 818). Walkers may climb to the summit of Graig Fawr (National Trust land), follow the old mineral railway track-bed below the scarp, or visit Gwaenysgor (Eagle and Child public house and shop) by a choice of attractive paths.

Clwyd County Council's Countryside Service publishes leaflets covering World's End, Eglwyseg Mountain and Moel Fammau Country Park, together with booklets covering way-marked walks connected to Offa's Dyke Path and the surrounding country. Details can be obtained from: The Countryside Centre, Loggerheads Country Park, Mold, CH7 5LH.

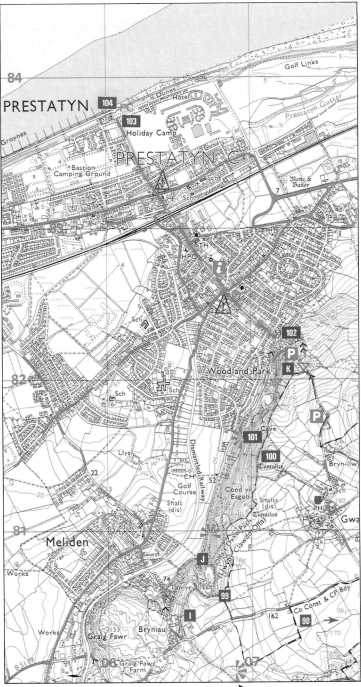

Contours are given in metres
The vertical interval is 5m

St Asaph (Llanelwy)

About 2½ miles (4 km) west of Rhuallt on the A55, St Asaph is a delightful miniature city. The cathedral is the smallest in Wales or England, but it is an ancient episcopal foundation, not a 'jumped-up parish church', and has an appropriately dignified aura. Most of the present building was constructed between 1284 and 1381 after a fire had destroyed earlier work. The North Wales Music Festival is held here every September.

Rhuddlan Castle, one of the strongest of Edward I's Welsh fortresses.

Rhuddlan

Rhuddlan, 4 miles (6.5 km) west on the A5151 from where the Path crosses, is noted for its remarkable castle. This was one of the series built by Edward I to consolidate his conquest of Wales. It was started in 1277 and consists of a strong walled and moated enclosure divided into inner and outer wards and there is a water tower by the Clwyd. There is a tradition that King Offa died here in 795.

Gop Hill 98

Gop Hill, north of the A5151, about 1½ miles (2.5 km) east of the Path, has a large burial mound on its summit and caves from which finds indicate early occupation. Low banks on the lower southern slopes were accepted by Sir Cyril Fox (1955) as being the ploughed-down remains of Offa's Dyke. Recent excavation has revealed no positive evidence and it must remain speculation whether the Dyke came this far north.

Prestatyn 102

Prestatyn is typical of the seaside resorts which sprang up all the way along the North Wales coast to serve the needs of the growing mass of holidaymakers from Merseyside and beyond. Paid holidays and cheap transport fuelled this boom in the early part of the 20th century. From the inland cliffs along which the Path approaches the town, spread below you are the acres of holiday camps and caravan sites, the patches of green devoted to sports and the miles of coast with pleasant bathing beaches. There are few buildings of historical interest; the main church, Christ Church, is entirely of the 19th and 20th centuries, but it has a pleasant setting standing back from the High Street in a green churchyard. The shops straggle over a considerable distance in the High Street and, north of the railway, along Bastion Road, and there is the appropriately wide range of cafés, entertainment and accommodation.

Although Prestatyn's appearance belongs to the heyday of seaside resorts, its site has been occupied from very early times, with finds from the Mesolithic and Neolithic periods and the excavation of the site of a Roman fort. There was an early medieval motte and bailey castle here but only scanty remains survive.

Sunset on the beach at Prestatyn, the northern end of a long journey.

128

PART THREE

USEFUL
INFORMATION

This section includes much information that relates to both the southern and northern guides to Offa's Dyke Path, since readers are likely to find this helpful when planning to walk the Path.

Transport

Visitors from large towns will be disappointed with what is available, but must remember the sparse population of the area. Some years ago a member of a party we were leading asked why we needed to rush to catch a particular bus at the end of a walk: 'Can't we get the next one?' 'Same time next week' had to be the reply! Services have not improved since.

In general you can use public transport to get to and from many points on the Path, but services are usually too limited to be of much help for travel between the end of a day's walk and overnight accommodation elsewhere, except from Chepstow to Monmouth and Buttington to Llanymynech. In addition, services do come and go and the deregulation policies on buses have made services less predictable than before: even operators covering a particular area can change.

The Offa's Dyke Association's annual *Where to Stay* guide has a section on public transport which, though it does not give timetables, does provide accurate lists of operators and contact points as at the start of each year. Such lists in a book with the life of this volume would only mislead, but some relevant key information follows.

Rail

There are six relevant lines (the nearest point to the Path is in capitals). Consult the current *British Rail Timetable*:

Birmingham–Gloucester–CHEPSTOW–Cardiff

Crewe–Shrewsbury–ABERGAVENNY (then catch a Hereford bus to PANDY)–Newport

Shrewsbury–KNIGHTON–Llanelli–Swansea (The Heart of Wales Line Travellers' Association, Frankville, Broad Street, Llandovery, Dyfed, SA20 0AR, fights hard to promote this rural line and is worth your support.)

Shrewsbury–WELSHPOOL (over 2 miles/3 km)–Aberystwyth

Wolverhampton–Shrewsbury–GOBOWEN–CHIRK (both over 2 miles/3 km)–Chester

Chester–PRESTATYN–Bangor–Holyhead (a frequent service)

Long-distance coaches

These serve Chepstow, Monmouth, Abergavenny, Kington, Welshpool, Oswestry, Chirk, Llangollen and Prestatyn. Services are seldom more than one a day, though there are often extra services in summer, and advance booking is needed. Interchange points such as Birmingham and Cheltenham mean that most services are accessible from towns in England, with through booking facilities. Your guide is the *National Express Timetable*: most libraries have copies, as do local bus operators who usually also act as booking agents.

Local buses

There are two separate but linked networks: the commercial services and supplementary services put out to tender to fill in the gaps. Companies can change, or withdraw, their own services at six weeks' notice. It is then up to the county council whether gaps thus created are filled. Subsidised services are reviewed annually. Thus, intending users must check the current position first with the Public Transport section of the appropriate county council (listed below), and possibly with the operators. No one operator has a monopoly on any part of the Path, though 'Red and White' is the major operator south of Monmouth as is 'Crosville' north of Welshpool.

County council Public Transport sections

Gloucestershire   – Gloucester (01452) 425609
Gwent   – Cwmbran (01633) 823478
Hereford & Worcester – 0345 125436 (local call rate)
Shropshire   – Shrewsbury 0345 056785 (local call rate)
Powys   – Llandrindod Wells (01597) 826642
Clwyd   – Mold (01352) 704035

The River Teme meandering through its valley, seen from Panpunton Hill abo

Knighton.

Accommodation

For a wide range of accommodation you are restricted to the major towns and tourist centres. For the northern half, the nearest are Knighton (on the Path), Clun (3miles/4.8 km off), Montgomery (1 mile/1.6 km), Welshpool (2 miles/3.2 km), Oswestry (2 miles), Chirk (1½ miles/2.4 km), Llangollen (1 mile), St Asaph (2½ miles/4 km) and Prestatyn (on the Path).

Several of the villages have an inn and a bed and breakfast establishment, but no greater choice. On or near the Path are Newcastle (half a mile/0.8 km), Forden, Buttington, Four Crosses, Llanymynech, Trefonen, Selattyn (1 mile), Froncysyllte, Trevor, Llandegla, Llanarmon-yn-Ial (1½ miles), Bodfari and Rhuallt.

However, except for the Clwydian Hills stretch, these are supplemented by many farms which have, over the years since the Path opened, catered for the needs of walkers.

Any accommodation list is history even before it is printed. Most up-to-date is the Offa's Dyke Association's annual *Where to Stay* guide (see address on page 139), which lists farms, hotels and guesthouses, transport facilities and other information.

Other useful annual lists, covering a wider geographical area, are those from:

Ramblers' Association, 1/5 Wandsworth Road, London, SW8 2XX. They are of course the umbrella organisation for walkers' interests and problems. Their Yearbook is available free to members (£2.95 to non-members), and indicates bed and breakfast accommodation near all national trails.

Wales Tourist Board, Brunel House, Fitzalan Road, Cardiff, CF2 1UY. Heart of England Tourist Board, Woodside, Larkhill Road, Worcester, WR5 2RF. Between them, the two Boards cover the Welsh and English sides of the Path.

Youth hostels

There are now (1995) only three relevant to the northern part of the Path (not equally spaced) at: Clun Mill (nearly 3½ miles/ 5.5 km from the Path), Llangollen (Tyndwr Hall, 2¾ miles/ 4.4 km) and Maeshafn (3¼ miles/5.2 km). Knighton (on route and in same building as the Offa's Dyke Centre) is currently (1995) closed pending structural repairs.

Further details, including membership of Youth Hostels Association, from Trevelyan House, 8 St Stephen's Hill, St Albans, Herts, AL1 2DY.

Camping

A few large permanent sites are quoted in the Offa's Dyke Association *Where to Stay* list but most walkers' camping is done, fairly informally, by arrangement with farms passed on the walk. The Association also publishes a separate *Camping List* which covers those farms where, at the time of publication, camping is permitted: this list is also updated regularly. Backpackers in particular are advised that they must not just camp anywhere: the permission of the farmer or other owner is absolutely essential.

Caravan sites and holiday lettings

Most mobile caravanners will be members of the Camping and Caravanning Club of Great Britain and Ireland, 11 Grosvenor Place, London, SW1W 0EY, whose excellent directory gives information on sites available. The accommodation guides referred to above all include sections on caravans and holiday homes let for self-catering.

Cycling and horseriding

Offa's Dyke Path is a footpath with several hundred stiles. There are few sections of any length that are bridleways and thus suitable for horseriders or cyclists: those that exist have been marked on the maps. There are no usable sections of any length on the northern half of the route.

Equipment

Compared with, say, the Pennine Way, Offa's Dyke is an 'easy' walk seldom far from town or village. Thus the need to carry enough equipment for emergencies to cover walking the whole route is reduced. Nevertheless the usual walker's rules of proper waterproofs, emergency warm clothing and rations, compass and whistle are sensible, especially over the moorland sections. Light walking boots are the all-purpose footwear: those who have a car or are doing day walks might like to have trainers, and also wellingtons, available to suit particular weather conditions.

Overall, travel as lightly loaded as safety allows as this will ease your way over the numerous stiles along the Path. For the backpacker there are enough shops *en route* for you to buy food and other provisions rather than carry all your needs from the start. Buying locally helps the local economy and is one way of showing your appreciation of the countryside.

Facilities for walkers

It is impracticable to list every shop and other useful facility in the text, and you should refer to the maps where useful features are indicated (although, in some cases, things may have changed since the maps were prepared). These include public transport, inns, cafés, shops and post offices, phone boxes, public toilets, picnic sites and information centres. Some car parking is indicated but, for obvious reasons, not the sort of spot where one car can just be squeezed on to a verge. Concentration has been on the route itself but, where we could, we have also noted towns, villages and access points a little way off. Medical services, banks and also a range of shops are to be found only in the towns: many staying open quite late. Elsewhere there are only the village shops, but the range of goods in these should not be underestimated. Most inns now serve food.

Early closing days in the major centres are:

Tuesday	– Hay-on-Wye
Wednesday	– Chepstow, Tintern, Kington, Knighton and Clun
Thursday	– Monmouth, Abergavenny, Presteigne, Welshpool, Oswestry, Chirk, Llangollen, Ruthin, Mold, Denbigh, St Asaph, Rhuddlan and Prestatyn
Saturday	– Montgomery

Visiting places of interest

The text of the book has tried to indicate the range of what is worth seeing a little off the route as well as on it. Towns, castles and abbeys are described in the features and circular walks, and the relevant tourist boards (referred to under 'Accommodation' above) have guide literature on the wider areas, of which the Offa's Dyke Path forms only a small part.

The principal ancient monuments are in the care of: (England) English Heritage, Fortress House, Savile Row, London, W1X 2HE, and (Wales) Cadw (Welsh Historic Monuments), Brunel House, 2 Fitzalan Road, Cardiff, CF2 1UY, both of which publish annual lists of opening times and charges.

The National Trust, 36 Queen Anne's Gate, London, SW1H 9AS is responsible for the Kymin and Powis and Chirk Castles. Their handbook gives opening times and a wealth of other information about all their properties.

Offa's Dyke Association

The Offa's Dyke Association was set up in 1969 by the late Frank Noble, MBE, to campaign for the opening of the Path. It has continued ever since as a body linking walkers, conservationists and historians and those who live and work locally – and are affected by the tourism created by the Path. Nearly 30,000 callers and correspondents are dealt with each year at their office in Knighton: mainly people seeking practical help and information concerned with walking the Path and local amenities. A range of its own specialist guides, maps, accommodation lists and equipment is produced and is complemented by a range of commercial products. The office is open daily from Easter to end of October, and weekdays (and some weekends) in winter.

Apart from this, the Association is active in Path maintenance and problems, and in conserving the natural and historical environment in which it exists. It manages the Offa's Dyke Centre in Knighton which provides information on the whole Path and for the town, and an exhibition on Offa and his Dyke. The Path Management staff work from the same building. It is hoped that the Youth Hostel on the premises will reopen after structural repairs. The Association is a membership body: its work is mainly dependent on its volunteers and on income from subscriptions and sales. It would welcome all Dyke-walkers to join its 1,000-strong band.

Its publication/sales list and membership form are available from Offa's Dyke Association (CC), West Street, Knighton, Powys, LD7 1EW. Please enclose a SAE.

Other organisations

Many other organisations are concerned with aspects of the Welsh Marches, the Dyke and Path. The roles of the Ramblers' Association, as the national body for walkers' interests, of the YHA and of the tourist boards have been mentioned above, under 'Accommodation', and of English Heritage, Cadw and the National Trust under 'Visiting places of interest'.

The Countryside Council for Wales and the Countryside Commission are responsible for National Trails (see page 23). Their addresses are Plas Penrhos, Ffordd Penrhos, Bangor, Gwynedd, LL57 2LQ, and John Dower House, Crescent Place, Cheltenham, GL50 3RA respectively. Path maintenance is carried out for them by the local county councils.

The Clwyd-Powys Archaeological Trust, 7a Church Street, Welshpool, Powys, SY21 7DL and Manchester University Extra-Mural Department, The University, Manchester, M13 9PL have been the most active bodies in recent years in archaeological work on the Dyke.

Council for the Protection of Rural England (CPRE), 4 Hobart Place, London, SW1W 0HY and CPRW, its Welsh counterpart, Ty Gwyn, 31 High Street, Welshpool, Powys, SY21 7JP work in the fields their titles suggest.

Most counties now have conservation or wildlife trusts. A full list can be obtained from the Royal Society for Nature Conservation, The Green, Witham Park, Waterside South, Lincoln, LN5 7JR. These include the Shropshire Wildlife Trust, 167 Frankwell, Shrewsbury, and the Montgomeryshire Wildlife Trust, 20 Severn Street, Welshpool, mentioned in the text in relation to the Jones's Rough reserve (page 70) and the Montgomery Canal (page 66).

The Inland Waterways Association, 114 Regent's Park Road, London, NW1 8UG is the umbrella organisation for restoration of canals, such as the Montgomery. The Woodland Trust, Autumn Park, Dysart Road, Grantham, Lincs, NG31 6LL promotes, and owns, amenity woodland, including several sections on Offa's Dyke Path. The Royal Society for the Protection of Birds (RSPB), The Lodge, Sandy, Beds, SG19 2DL is what its title says.

The Ordnance Survey, Romsey Road, Maybush, Southampton, SO16 4GU is the national mapping organisation.

Bibliography

Choosing books for further reading is invidious: what follows is what we, over many years, have found useful and entertaining.

Path guides

Noble, Frank, *Offa's Dyke Path* (Offa's Dyke Association, 1981): by the man who did so much to bring the Path into being.

Richards, Mark, *Through Welsh Border Country following Offa's Dyke Path* (Thornhill, 1976): a 'Wainwright'-style hand-drawn guide.

Wright, Christopher, *A Guide to Offa's Dyke Path* (Constable, 1986, 2nd edition): very detailed on towns and monuments on or near the Path.

Welsh Border generally

Fraser, Maxwell, *Welsh Border Country* (Batsford, 1972).

Millward, R. and Robinson, A., *The Welsh Border* (Eyre Methuen, 1978).

Stanford, S. C., *Archaeology of the Welsh Marches* (revised edition, 1991, published by the Author).

Dyke archaeology

Fox, Sir Cyril, *Offa's Dyke* (British Academy, 1955): a detailed account of the key 1920s/30s survey.

Hill, David, articles in *Mediaeval Archaeology* on the recent work by Manchester University Extra-Mural Department.

Noble, Frank, edited by Gelling, M., *Offa's Dyke Reviewed* (BAR British Series 114, 1983): the most thorough modern analysis of the Dyke.

Stenton, Sir Frank, *Anglo Saxon England* (Oxford University Press, 1943, 3rd edition 1971) is the best comprehensive guide to the history of the period.

Trueman, A. E., *Geology and Scenery in England and Wales* (Penguin, 1949) is the best and simplest exponent on this topic.

Buildings

The Penguin *Buildings of England and Wales* series, edited and mostly written by Sir Nikolaus Pevsner, is unbeatable. Relevant volumes are those on Gloucestershire: the Vale and Forest of Dean, Herefordshire, Shropshire, Clwyd and Powys. There is no Gwent volume yet: we found Bobby Freeman's *Gwent* (Robin Clark, 1980) useful. For specific properties in their care the guides of Cadw, English Heritage and the National Trust are essential.

Alternative relevant paths

'Castles' Alternative': Monmouth to Hay, and 'Knighton Circuits' are devised by Offa's Dyke Association, which has booklets on each.

Glyndwr's Way: Knighton to Machynlleth and back to Welshpool, is covered by a set of leaflets from Powys County Council and Richard Sale, *Owain Glyndwr's Way* (New edition, Constable 1992). This route is currently (1995) being considered for upgrading to National Trail status.

'Period' books

Borrow, George, *Wild Wales* (Everyman Library): an 1861 travel book.

Hogg, Garry, *And Far Away* (Dent, 1946): the first book about walking the Dyke, well before the existence of Offa's Dyke Path.

Kilvert's Diary, edited by Plomer, W. (Jonathan Cape, 1964; Penguin, reissued 1984): this one-volume selection is a good sample of the now-famous evocative mid-Victorian description of life in the Clyro/Hay area.

Mabinogion, The (Everyman Library): the source book for Welsh legends.

Watkins, Alfred, *The Old Straight Track* (Abacus, 1974): an exposition of one theory about many of our ancient monuments.

Fiction

Chatwin, Bruce, *On the Black Hill* (Jonathan Cape, 1982; Picador, 1983): now a film and play too.

Williams, Raymond, *Border Country* (Chatto & Windus, 1960): life between the Wars in the East Wales valleys.

The historical novels of Edith Pargeter, such as *The Heaven Tree*, and *The Secret of Grey Walls* and other children's stories by Malcolm Saville, are relevant and evocative of the Welsh Borders, as is the verse of A. E. Housman in *A Shropshire Lad*.

Other

Davies, Dewi, *Welsh Place Names and Their Meaning* (Cambrian Press).

Rees, W., *A Historical Atlas of Wales* (Faber & Faber, 1951).

There are many excellent guides and histories to particular towns and areas, and volumes on canal and railway history, but space does not allow more than a passing reference to these topics.

Ordnance Survey Maps covering the Offa's Dyke Path
(*listed from north to south*)
Landranger Maps: 116,117,126,137,148,161,162
Pathfinder Maps: 737(SJ08/18), 755(SJ07/17), 772(SJ06/16)
788(SJ05/15), 789(SJ25/35), 806(SJ24/34)
827(SJ23/33), 847(SJ22/32), 868(SJ21/31)
888(SJ20/30), 909(SO29/39), 930(SO28/38)
950(SO27/37), 971(SO26/36), 993(SO25/35)
1016(SO24/34), 1039(SO23/33), 1063(SO22/32)
1086(SO21/31), 1087(SO41/51), 1111(SO40/50)
1131(ST49/59).
Outdoor Leisure Maps: Map 13, Brecon Beacons-Eastern; Map 14, Forest of Dean and Wye Valley.
Motoring Maps: Reach Offa's Dyke Path using Travelmaster Map 7, Wales.

Glossary of Welsh place names

Welsh place names are usually descriptions, some of them quite poetic. But the emphasis is on description. Many places begin with the word *aber*, meaning the mouth of a river. Aberystwyth, the mouth of Ystwyth River; Abertawe (the Welsh name for Swansea), the mouth of the Tawe River. Another class of place name begins with the word *llan*, a church or parish. Llanfair, the church of (St) Mary; Llanfihangel, the church of (St) Michael.

Plurals in Welsh are usually formed by adding the letters AU to the end of a word. An example is *dol* (a meadow); *dolau* (meadows).

A small Welsh–English pocket dictionary would be a useful companion in any walker's rucksack. But for the impecunious here is a small glossary of common words and their meanings:

Bach, fach, small	*Dyffryn,* valley
Bryn, hill	*Llyn,* lake
Bwlch, pass	*Llys,* hall or palace
Caer, gaer, fort	*Maen,* stone
Cefn, ridge	*Mawr, fawr,* big
Clawdd, dyke	*Melin,* mill
Coed, wood	*Nant,* stream
Du, black	*Pont,* bridge
Dwr, water	*Ty,* house